From Bull Run
to Appomattox

LUTHER W. HOPKINS.
Taken from an old daguerreotype in 1861,
before entering the army.

From Bull Run
to Appomattox

The Recollections of a Confederate Army
Trooper of Company 'A', Sixth Virginia Cavalry
During the American Civil War

Luther W. Hopkins

LEONAUR

From Bull Run to Appomattox
The Recollections of a Confederate Army Trooper of Company 'A',
Sixth Virginia Cavalry During the American Civil War
by Luther W. Hopkins

First published under the title
From Bull Run to Appomattox

Leonaur is an imprint of Oakpast Ltd

ISBN: 978-0-85706-643-5 (hardcover)
ISBN: 978-0-85706-644-2 (softcover)

http://www.leonaur.com

Publisher's Notes

The opinions of the authors represent a view of events in which he
was a participant related from his own perspective,
as such the text is relevant as an historical document.

The views expressed in this book are not necessarily
those of the publisher.

Contents

Preface   7

From Harper's Ferry to Bull Run   11

From Bull Run to Seven Pines   25

From Bull Run to Seven Pines (Continued)   31

From Seven Pines to Antietam   36

From Antietam to Chancellorsville   45

From Chancellorsville to Gettysburg   64

From Gettysburg to the Wilderness   79

From the Wilderness to James River   96

From James River to Petersburg   113

From Petersburg to Appomattox and Home   127

An After-Thought   137

Preface

Life is the mirror of the king and slave,
'Tis just what you are and do.
Then give to the world the best you have,
And the best will come back to you.

I never thought that I should be guilty of writing a book. I did not, however, do this with malice aforethought. My son is responsible for whatever sin I may have committed in presenting this to the public. He and I have been good friends ever since we became acquainted, and he has always insisted upon my telling him all that I know. When he was about three years old he discovered that I had been a soldier in Lee's army from 1861 to 1865, and, although he is of Quaker descent and a loyal member of the Society of Friends, and I am half Quaker, yet he loved war stories and I loved to tell them. This accounts for the production of the book. After I had told him these stories over and over, again and again, when he was grown he insisted upon my starting at the beginning and giving him the whole of my experience in the Confederate army. Then he wanted it published. I yielded to his request, and here is the book. This is not, however, an exact copy of the typewritten manuscript which he has. The original manuscript is more personal. I thought the change would make it more acceptable to the general reader.

We all believe in peace; universal peace, but when war does come, and such a costly war as the one from which this story is taken, we ought to get all the good out of it we can. The long marches along dusty roads, under hot suns, the long marches through sleet and snows, the long dreary nights without shelter, the march of the picket to and fro on his beat, the constant drilling and training, the struggle on the battlefields, all these are part of the material that the world has always used in constructing a nation. While there are some things about war that we should forget, there are many things that ought never to be forgotten, but should be handed down from sire to son all through the ages that are to come.

Historians have told us much about our Civil War, but they have left out the part that appeals most to the boy, and it is this part that I have tried to bring before the public. Men may read the book if they will, but it is written more particularly for the youth. The boy of today and the boy that is yet to be ought to know of the bloody sweat through which this nation passed in reaching its present position among the great nations of the earth, and the part the boy played in it. It is said that one boy is a boy; two boys a half boy and three boys no boy at all. That may be true of the boy running loose, unbridled like a colt, but gather up these boys and train them, harness and hitch them and they will move the world or break a trace. It is the boy who decides the fate of nations. I don't know the average age of our soldiers in times of peace, but when wars come and there is a call for soldiers, it is mainly the boy in his teens who responds; yet, strange to say, the historian has never thought it worthwhile to put much emphasis upon what the boy does in the upbuilding of a nation.

Another thing that has been neglected by the historian is the brave and noble part the horse took in our war. The grays, the bays, the sorrels, the roans, the chestnuts, have not been forgotten in this story. Indeed, as I have already said, I have tried to bring to light that part of the story of our Civil War that has not been told.

Now, young men and boys, girls too, old men, if there are any, read this book, all of you, regardless of geographical lines, for I have tried to be fair to those who wore the blue. As the years go by, I have learned to respect and love those who fought for the

Union. I visited Boston and its environments two summers ago for the first time. During the visit, I never met a person whom I had ever seen before, yet all the time that I was away I felt at home. I said to myself, are these the people we of the South used to hate? Are these the people that we once mobbed as they marched through our streets? Yes, they are the same people or their descendants, but then we did not know them and they did not know us. I came back feeling proud of my country, and I only wish I could give here a detailed account of that visit. If, early in the spring of 1861, the North and South had swapped visits, each party would have gone home singing, "there ain't goin' to be no war," but we had a war; a great war, a costly war; let us forget what ought to be forgotten and remember what ought to be remembered. I want to pay this tribute to the Northern soldiers. I have discovered this: When two armies of equal numbers met face to face in the open, it was nearly always a toss up as to who would win. Numbers don't always count in battle. General Hooker, with his army of 130,000, retreating before Lee's 60,000, doesn't mean that one rebel could whip two yankees. It only meant that "Fighting Joe" had more than he could manage. His numbers were an encumbrance. There were other differences which, for the sake of brevity, I will not mention, but will add this one word: One bluecoat was all I cared to face, and I believe every other Johnny Reb will say the same.

May we never have another war, but boys, remember this: "Peace hath her victories, no less renowned than war," and the boy that wishes to count in this world must *train*. But there are other training schools quite as helpful as the camp and the battlefield.

Luther W. Hopkins.

Baltimore, November, 1908.

Gen. Joseph E. Johnston,
Who preceded Gen. Robert E. Lee in
command of the Army of Northern Virginia.

CHAPTER 1

From Harper's Ferry to Bull Run

O war, thou hast thy fierce delight,
Thy gleams of joy intensely bright;
Such gleams as from thy polished shield
Fly dazzling o'er the battlefield.

Is there a boy in all this wide land, North or South, who would not like to hear what a boy has to say of his experience as a private soldier in the Confederate Army from 1861 to 1865, serving for the most part in Stuart's Cavalry of Lee's army? Men have told their story, and graphically told it from a man's standpoint. But who has spoken for the boy? Who has told of the part the boy played in that great drama that was on the stage for four years without intermission? That bloody drama in which there were 3,000,000 players—a play that cost the country eight billions in money and half a million human lives?

I do not know how it was in the Northern armies, but the bulk of Lee's soldiers in the ranks were boys in their teens. It was these boys who made Thomas Jonathan Jackson, "Stonewall Jackson;" who put Robert E. Lee's name in the hall of fame and who lifted J.E.B. Stuart up to the rank of lieutenant-general of cavalry. One of these boys has written the story as he remembers it in plain, simple language; not a history, but simply an account of what he saw and did while this eventful history was being made. If his experience is different from others, or does not accord in all respects with what the historian has written, it is because we do not all see alike. The writer has not consulted the histories for material for this story; he did not have to do this. If all the boys who served in the Confederate Army were to write their experience, they would all be different, yet all approximately correct, and perhaps, taken together, would be the most perfect history that could be written of the Confederate side of the Civil War.

In the early spring of 1861 I was seventeen years old and going to school about half a mile from my home in Loudoun county, Virginia. Twelve miles distant was Harper's Ferry, where four years previous John Brown had made an attempt to raise an insurrection among the slaves in that district. He seized the United States arsenal, located there, for the purpose of arming the negroes, who were expected to flock to his standard and have their freedom declared. The negroes did not respond; John Brown and a few of his followers were captured and hanged. This atrocious act of Brown and his abettors kindled a flame in the hearts of the Southern people that led to the Civil War. But none felt it so keenly as did the Virginians, because it was their sacred soil that had been traduced. Three years previous to this, when I was ten years of age, I remember to have heard a political discussion among a body of men, and the following words have lingered in my memory ever since, and they are all that I can recall of their talk: "If there is a war between the North and South, Virginia will be the battlefield."

I thought it would be grand, and waited anxiously for the fulfilment of this prophecy. Then when John Brown swooped down on Harper's Ferry with his cohorts, it looked as if the day had really come and that the prediction was about to be fulfilled. From that time war talk was general, especially among the small boys. But the intense excitement caused by the Brown episode gradually abated. It broke out afresh, however, when later it was announced that Abraham Lincoln was elected President of the United States. It seemed to be the consensus of opinion that the result would be war, and that Virginia in truth would be the battleground, and that the counties along the Potomac would receive the first shock of battle. We boys of Loudoun county, right on the Potomac, felt that we were "it," and we had a kind of pity for those poor fellows a little farther back. We were in the front row, and when the curtain went up we could see and hear everything. There were about thirty boys attending our school between the ages of fifteen and twenty. They all entered the Confederate Army, but few survived the war.

Before going on with the story, perhaps I ought to explain why these boys were so eager for war, when they knew that the enemy would be their own countrymen. There was a peculiar relationship existing between the slave owner's family and the slaves that the North never did and never will understand. On the part of the white children it was love, pure and simple, for the slave, while on the part of the adult it was more than friendship, and, I might add, the feeling was reciprocated by the slaves. The children addressed the adult blacks as Uncle and Aunt, and treated them with as much respect as they did their blood relatives. It was Uncle Reuben and Aunt Dinah.

The adult white also addressed the older coloured people in the same way. With but few exceptions, the two races lived together in perfect harmony. If a slave-owner was cruel to his slaves, it was because he was a cruel man, and all who came in contact with him, both man and beast, suffered at his hands. Even his children did not escape. These men are found everywhere. The old black mammy, with her head tied up in a white cloth, was loved, respected and honoured by every inmate of the home, regardless of colour.

The following incident will be of interest: Hon. John Randolph Tucker, one of Virginia's most gifted and learned sons, who represented his State in the U.S. Senate, always celebrated his birthday. I remember to have attended one of these celebrations. It was shortly after the close of the war. Mr. Tucker was then between fifty-five and sixty years of age. He had grown children. Fun making was one of his characteristics. On these annual occasions, it was his custom to dress himself in a long white gown and bring into the parlour his old black nurse, whom he called "mammy." She sat in her rocking-chair with her head tied up in the conventional snow-white cloth. Mr. Tucker, dressed up as a child in his nightgown, would toddle in and climb up into her lap, and she would lull him to sleep with an old-time nursery song, no doubt one of her own compositions. This could not possibly have occurred had the skin of his nurse been white.

When a daughter married and set up her own home, fortunate was she if she took with her the mammy. In many homes the slaves were present at family prayers. The kitchen and the cabin furnished the white children places of resort that were full of pleasure.

This was the relation between white and coloured as I remember it from a child in my part of Virginia. And tonight, as I write these lines, while the clock tolls off the hour of eleven, I cannot keep out of my mind the words of that little poem by Elizabeth Akers:

> Backward, turn backward, oh time in thy flight,
> And make me a child again, just for tonight.

How anyone could have desired to break up this happy relationship was beyond the conception of the child, and more or less incomprehensible to the adult.

Somewhere between childhood and youth we children all learned that there was a race of people up North called Abolitionists, who were so mean that they sent secret agents through the country to persuade the coloured people to leave their homes and go North, where they could be free. That these agents were disguised as peddlers or otherwise, and that they visited the cabins of the slaves during the late hours of the night, and went so far as to urge them to rise up in a body and declare their freedom, and if necessary to murder those who held them as slaves. This delusion, if it were a delusion, might have been dispelled had not John Brown and his men appeared upon the scene to give an ocular demonstration of their real intent. The few men with him may have been the only following that he had, but the damage had been done. Virginia was fighting mad. What had been whispered about the abolitionists in secret was now pro-

JEFFERSON C. DAVIS.
President of the Confederate States of
America. Taken just before his
inauguration.

claimed from the housetops. John Brown was an abolitionist, and all abolitionists were John Browns, so the youths at least reasoned. The words abolitionist and Yankee were for the most part synonymous terms; the former being hard to pronounce, the child usually employed the latter. Some of the young children did not know that a Yankee was a human being, as the following incident will illustrate:

When the first Federal soldiers entered the village of Middleburg, Loudoun county, Virginia, the cry went up and down the streets, "The Yankees have come!" The streets were soon deserted by every living thing except the dogs and the ubiquitous, irrepressible small boy, who was or pretended to be "skeered o' nothin'." This war was gotten up for his special benefit, and he was determined to see all that was to be seen, and was always to be found well up in front. The women and children within their homes crowded to the windows to see the cavalry as it marched by. A little three-year old nephew of mine, with the expression of alarm disappearing from his face, said: "Mamma, them ain't Yankees, them's soldiers." He expected to see some kind of hideous animal.

This is the education the Virginia boys got, who afterward became Lee's soldiers. They were brought up in this school, and when they became soldiers, wearing the gray, they felt that they had something to fight for. They believed that they were real patriots, notwithstanding they were called rebels and traitors.

This brings us to the beginning of the Civil War, or at least to the secession movement. Lincoln had not yet taken his seat as President, when several of the Southern States seceded and formed a Southern Confederacy, with Montgomery, Ala., as the capital, and Jefferson C. Davis as President. This was recognized by the United States Government as open rebellion, and as soon as Mr. Lincoln took the reins of government, he called for 75,000 troops to suppress the rebellion.

Virginia must either furnish her quota of troops or withdraw from the Union. She promptly chose the latter, and shortly afterward became a part of the Southern Confederacy. As soon as the ordinance of secession had passed the Virginia Legislature, there were a thousand Paul Reveres in the saddle, carrying the news to every point not reached by telegraph lines. The young men and boys did not wait for the call from the Governor. Military companies, infantry, cavalry and artillery sprang up everywhere. Anyone who chose and could get a sufficient following might raise a company. These companies were offered to the Governor and promptly accepted. The ordinance of secession was passed at night. The next morning Virginia troops were on their way to seize Harper's Ferry.

On the approach of these troops the small guard of United States soldiers stationed there set fire to the buildings and fled. The fire was extinguished by the citizens, I think, and much of the valuable machinery and military stores was saved. The machinery was sent to Richmond, and the arms were used in equipping the soldiers. Harper's Ferry became one of the outposts of the Confederacy, and a place of rendezvous for the rapidly-growing Confederate battalions. Thomas Jonathan Jackson, afterward known as Stonewall Jackson, was sent to Harper's Ferry to drill and organize the forces gathering there, into an army. He was later superseded by Gen. Jos. E. Johnston, but Jackson remained as a subordinate commander. In the meantime, the Confederate Government had demanded that Gen. Anderson evacuate Fort Sumter, at the entrance of Charleston harbour, and also had said, if not in words, in action, to the Government at Washington as it saw United States armies gathering near its northern frontier, So far shalt thou come, and no further.

But to go back to the thirty boys. What were they doing all this time? Just prior to the date of Virginia's secession they were gathering in groups at noon and recess, on the way to and from school, and talking war. How big and important we seemed as we prospectively saw ourselves dressed as soldiers, armed and keeping step to the beat of the drum. There was but little studying, for our preceptor was not hard on us. He had once been a boy himself, and appreciating the conditions that surrounded us, he chiefly employed himself in keeping the school together until hostilities began, if it should really come to that. I don't know how long the school continued, but I do know that these particular boys were early on the drill ground, and were being trained into soldiers. It was difficult for the parents to keep the fourteen and fifteen-year-old boys at home or in school. I had a brother sixteen years old who was first of the family to enlist, and then all followed, one after another, until four of us were in the ranks.

There were mature men and old men, men of heavy responsibilities, who saw farther into the future than the younger generation. These went about with bowed heads and talked seriously of what the future might bring. They wisely discussed constitutional law, State rights, what foreign nations would have to say about it, the nations that had to have our cotton. "Cotton was king," they said, and the South owned the king, soul and body. Questions like these were discussed among the men, but like one of old, the boy cared for none of these things. In the language of a famous Union general, his place was to meet the enemy and defeat him. I remember about this time hearing this toast being offered to the South:

"May her old men make her laws, her young men fight her battles, and her maidens spin her cotton."

The boy well understood the part he was to play, and he was in his element, and as happy as a boy could be. I cannot remember just when the first call was made for troops by the Governor, but I do know, as I have already stated, that the boys heard the call from a higher source, and they were coming from mountain and plain, from hillside and valley, from the shop, and office and school. Well do I recall the joy that welled up in every boy's breast as one after another of the actors took their places on the stage. Again I find myself quoting Elizabeth Akers, this time substituting a word:

Backward, turn backward, oh time in thy flight,
And make me a BOY again, just for tonight.

Now let us take a peep into the Virginia homes. What were

the women doing? Ah, they were as busy as bees. These boys must be equipped not only with munitions of war, but each boy must take with him as many home comforts as could possibly be compressed into a bundle small enough to be carried. When he was at home it took a good-sized room to hold these things; now he must put them into his pocket or on his back, and it took all of a mother's skill to gather these things up into the least possible space, that her boy might have in the camp life all that a mother's love could give him.

The Government would furnish the guns, the powder, the lead, the canteen and knapsack and haversack; the tin-shop, the tin-cup; the shoemaker, the boots; the bookstore, the Bible (every boy must carry a Bible), but all the clothing, all the little necessary articles for comfort and health, must be manufactured in the home. Did you ever open the outside casing of one of these large patent beehives and see the bees at work inside? What rushing and pushing and confusion! Every bee, so far as human eye can see, seems busy. This beehive was but a replica of a Virginia home in the spring of 1861.

While these things were going on in the home the boys were drilling in the field, for they were now out of school. All were anxious to get their equipment, and to be the first to offer their services to the Governor.

Had these boys any conception of what they were rushing into? Suppose just at this time the curtain had been lifted, and they could have seen Bull Run and Seven Pines, Manassas and Sharpsburg, Fredericksburg and Chancellorsville, Gettysburg and The Wilderness, Spotsylvania, Cold Harbor and Appomattox? And if they could have seen a picture of their homes and fields as they appeared in 1865, would they have rushed on? Perhaps I can answer that question by pointing to the battlefield of New Market. In the fall of 1864, after nearly all the great battles had been fought, the young cadets from Lexington, Va., who had not yet been under fire, but with a full knowledge of what war meant, rushed into this battle like veterans and were mowed down as grain, their little bodies lying scattered over the field like sheaves of wheat.

> *O war, thou hast thy fierce delight,*
> *Thy gleams of joy intensely bright;*
> *Such gleams as from thy polished shield*
> *Fly dazzling o'er the battlefield.*

Yes, war has its bright, attractive side, and those boys, as I knew them, would have looked at these moving-pictures as they came one after another into view, and then perhaps have turned pale; perhaps they would have shuddered and then cried out, "On with the dance; let joy be unconfined;" and it was literally on with the dance. School, as I have just said, was out, and every laddie had his lassie, and you may be sure they improved the time. It was drill through the day and dance through the night.

> *No sleep till morn when youth and pleasure meet*
> *To chase the glowing hours with flying feet.*

The boys were happy, and "*all went merry as a marriage bell*," and well that it was so. When we looked into the hive we saw that the bees were busy, but as far as human eye could discover, there was no head; all was confusion; it was pushing and shoving and coming and going, and one might have asked the question, What are they doing? What does it all mean? If we could have seen farther into the hive we would have discovered that back of this busy throng sat the queen, and that these were her subjects, doing her bidding. She was sending out her little rogues to rob the flowers, and they were coming back richly laden with spoils. This was the raw material, and it was being worked up. When the season was over and the flowers were dead, and we drew from the hive the finished product, so perfect in all its parts and richly stored with sweetened treasures, we began to realize that there was a master mind behind it all.

Do you suppose for a moment that when these young men and boys of Virginia, in fact from all over the South, who were rushing with such intense enthusiasm in the Confederate ranks, these fathers and mothers and sisters, who were equipping these youths with comforts without which they could not have endured the hardships of the camp, do you suppose they were but following the dictates of a few maddened, fire-eating fanatics, and that the whole would end in debt, death and desolation? If you had lived in 1861 you might have been excused for thinking so. But what do you think of it today, as the finished product begins to unfold itself to our view? Do you not believe there was a master mind behind it all, a King, and that these boys were but part of His royal subjects, doing His will?

Suppose there had been no rush and no adequate army at Bull Run to meet McDowell and his forces as they came marching out from Washington with flying colours? Suppose the Confederates had been beaten at Bull Run and Richmond had fallen, and the war had ended then? What miserable creatures we poor devils of the South would have been! The world would have laughed at us. We would have lost all of our self-respect. A cycle of time could not have wiped out our self-contempt, and God might have said, "I cannot build up a great nation with material like this." The North would have had no Grand Army Veterans, and no deeds of heroism with which to keep alive the fire of patriotism in the hearts of their children. Spain in 1898 might have successfully defied us, and China and Japan have roamed at will over our land. No; the war was a necessity. It was costly, but was worth all that it cost. It has made of us a very great nation.

Now I shall go back and tell how it was done. I will do so by narrating my own experience, and as my experience, with but slight variation, was the experience of every boy who served in the Confederate army, the reader will have a fair idea of what the boy's life was during those four years.

The firing upon Fort Sumter was like throwing a stone into a hornet's nest. All the North was aroused. Troops came pouring into Washington by every train. A Massachusetts regiment, in passing through the streets of Baltimore, was mobbed, and the song "Maryland, My Maryland" was wafted out on the air.

Maryland boys, under cover of night, were crossing the Potomac to help drive the invaders back. They came singing "The Despot's Heel is on Thy Shore." Rumours flew thick and

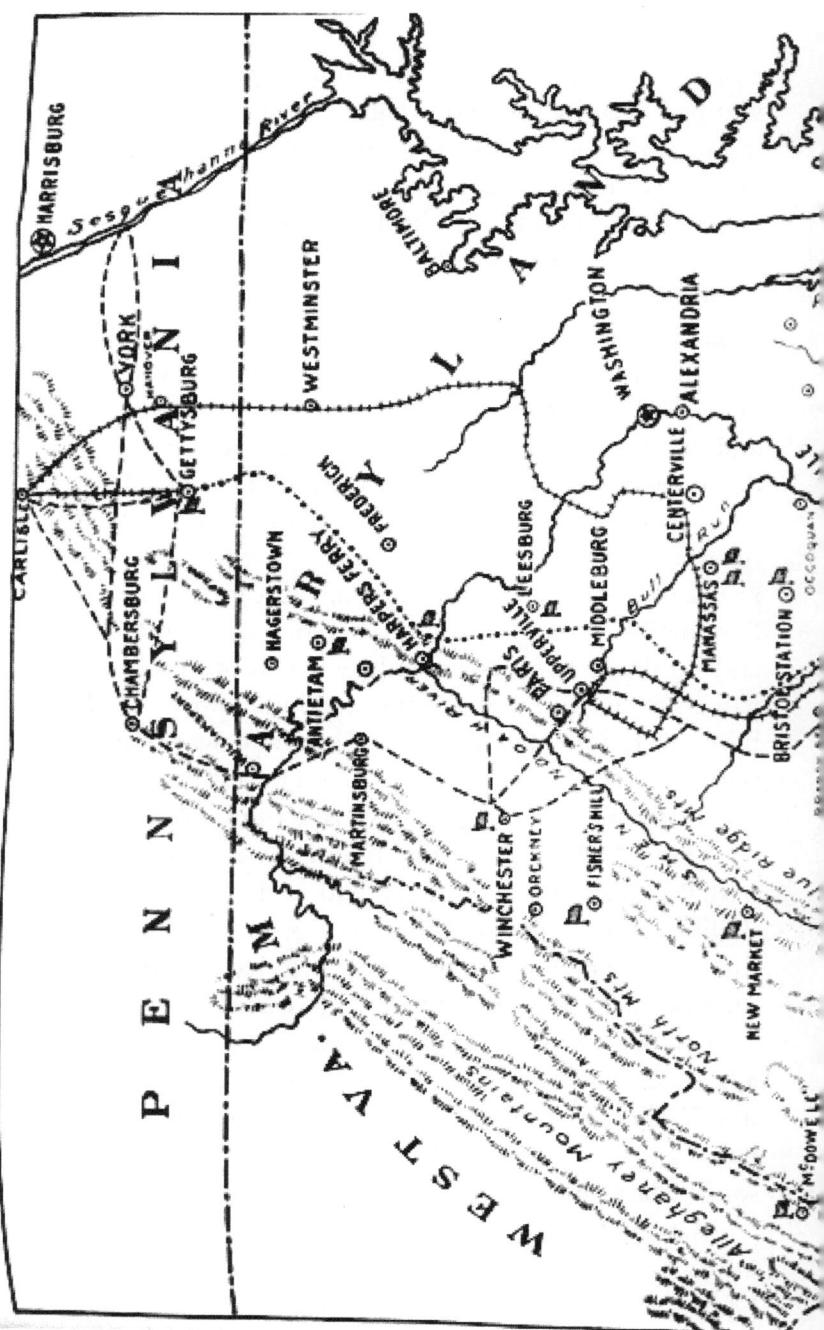

MAP SHOWING MARCH OF
UNION AND CONFEDERATE ARMIES
FROM THE RAPPAHANNOCK RIVER TO GETTYSBURG.

CONFEDERATE INFANTRY ————————
CAVALRY ————————
UNION ARMY ————————

PRINCIPAL BATTLEFIELDS

HARRISONBURG
CULPEPER
PORT REPUBLIC
STAUNTON
CHARLOTTESVILLE
CEDAR RUN
WILDERNESS
CHANCELLORS
FREDERICKSBURG
SPOTSYLVANIA
RICHMOND
SEVEN PINES
COLD HARBOR
PETERSBURG
APPOMATTOX

Rapidan
RAPPAHANNOCK RIVER
POTOMAC RIVER
SHENANDOAH RIVER
YORK RIVER
JAMES RIVER

fast. Now and then shots were exchanged between opposing pickets as they walked to and fro on the banks of the Potomac river that separated them. In fact, the curtain was up and the play had begun. Harper's Ferry, Leesburg and Manassas (see map)[1] became strategical points, and at each of these the Confederates were concentrating their forces.

By June 1, 1861, Jos. E. Johnston at Harper's Ferry had an army of 10,000. Gen. A.P. Hill at Leesburg, 3000. Gen P. G. T. Beauregard at Manassas, 12,000. These were Confederates. On the Union side, Gen. Patterson had an army of about 15,000 confronting Johnston, and McDowell at the head of 35,000 was crossing the Potomac at Washington *en route* for Bull Run.

---

1. The main battlefields are marked with a flag, but there are over 50 more; in fact, eliminating the rough mountain ranges, nearly every foot of Virginia soil covered by this map felt the tramp of the soldier and heard the hiss of the bullet.

Chapter 2

From Bull Run to Seven Pines

Only a boy! and his father had said
He never could let his youngest go;
Two already were lying dead
Under the feet of the trampling foe.

As the advance guard of the Federal army entered Alexandria, Va., on the south side of the Potomac, a Confederate flag was seen floating from the roof of a hotel kept by one Jackson. Col. Elsworth, commanding the advance force, hauled it down. Jackson shot him dead, and was in turn killed by Elsworth's soldiers. This, I believe, was the first blood shed on Virginia soil.

As McDowell moved his army toward Manassas, Johnston fell back toward Winchester, so as to be in a position to reinforce Beauregard if it became necessary.

Before McDowell had reached Fairfax Courthouse the greater portion of Johnston's army was *en route* for Manassas. So closely did Johnston conceal his movements that Patterson was not aware that Johnston had left his front until it was too late to follow him. The little army at Leesburg also marched rapidly to Manassas.

These united Confederate armies numbered about 27,000 men. McDowell's army, as I have stated, numbered 35,000.

In order to be prepared for an emergency, the Governor of Virginia had called the militia from the counties adjacent to Manassas to assemble at that place. That included my county. I joined the militia and marched to Manassas, arriving there a few days before the battle.

There was skirmishing for some days between the advanced forces of the two armies, but the real battle was fought on Sunday, July 21, 1861.

My command took no part in this battle, but it was in line of battle in the rear of the fighting forces, ready to take part if its services were needed.

Soldiers, like sailors, are superstitious. As the hour for the battle drew near, those of a mystical turn of mind saw, or thought they saw, a strange combination of stars in the heavens. Some said, "I never saw the moon look that way before." Clouds assumed mysterious shapes. Some saw in them marching armies, and other fearful phenomena. A strange dog was seen one night passing in and out the various camps into the officers' tents and out again as if he were numbering the men. This created no little comment. The dog was all unconscious of the excitement he was creating. He had simply lost his master, but his manner appeared ominous to those who were looking for the mystical. These are the kind of soldiers that run at the first fire. They are found in all armies.

I have always claimed that I am not superstitious, but I must admit that there is an atmosphere that hangs around the camp on the eve of an approaching battle that is well calculated to give one's imagination full play. The doctors examining their medical chests, packages of white bandages and lint arriving, the movement of the ambulances, the unusual number of litters that come into view, the chaplains a little more fervent in their prayers, officers, from the commanding general down to the lowest rank, more reserved and less approachable. Even the horses seem to be restive, or we imagine them to be so. In fact, everything takes on a different attitude. The very air appears to be laden with an indescribable something that makes every individual soldier feel himself lifted up into a position of responsibility quite different from the place he occupied when loitering around the camp with the enemy far away from the front.

This was the state of things as I saw them in and around

GEN. THOMAS JONATHAN JACKSON,
Christened "Stonewall Jackson" by General
Bee at the first Battle of Manassas.

Manassas on the eve of the first battle of Bull Run. Before the rising of the sun on that beautiful Sabbath day, July 21, 1861, the cannon could be heard in the distance, which told us that the two combatants had locked horns. All day long we could hear the booming of the guns and see the smoke of the battle over the tops of the low pines in our front, and I was ever so anxious to get closer and see the real thing, but soldiers cannot go just where they may desire, especially when a great battle is in progress.

Early in the day I saw what thrilled me no little. It was the first blood I had ever seen shed on a battlefield. I saw coming across the field, moving quite slowly, a man leading a horse. As they approached I saw that the horse was limping, and the man was a soldier. The horse was badly wounded and bleeding, and seemed to be in great pain. Whenever the man would stop the horse would attempt to lie down. I wanted to go to him and put my arms around his neck and tell him he was a hero. The man and the horse passed by, for there was too much going on to allow a single wounded horse to absorb all of one's attention.

Toward the afternoon news came in from the front that our army was beaten and was in full retreat.

Every available man was called from the camp, and a second line of defence was formed, behind which the retreating army could rally and make another stand. It was then that I began to realize what war was.

About five o'clock a soldier came across the field from the front with a gun on his shoulder. As he came up to our line someone asked him how the battle was going. He replied, "We've got them on the trot." Then there was wild cheering; the soldier was right. McDowell's army was beaten and in full retreat toward Washington. It proved to be the worst rout that any army suffered during the Civil War.

At one stage of the battle it looked very doubtful for our side. Beauregard believed that he was beaten, and had ordered his forces to fall back, calling on Johnston to cover his retreat. But the arrival of Elzey's brigade of Johnston's army upon the field just at this psychological moment turned the battle in our favour. A member of the First Maryland Regiment, forming a part of this brigade, has given me a graphic description of how the brigade was hurried from the railroad station at Manassas, across the fields for five miles under the hot July sun, the men almost famished for water and covered with dust, most of the distance at double-quick, toward the firing line, from which the panic-stricken Confederates were fleeing in great disorder.

But I shall only narrate what I saw myself, and will not quote farther, however interesting it may be. A train came down from Richmond about three o'clock, bringing the President of the Confederacy, Jefferson C. Davis, and fresh troops, but they arrived too late to be of any special service. I saw the President as he mounted a gray horse, with a number of other prominent Confederates from Richmond, and move off toward the battlefield.

A short time after this they began to bring in the wounded from the front. I stood by and saw the pale face and glassy eyes of Gen. Bee as they took him dying from the ambulance and carried him into a house near the Junction. It was he who an hour or so before had said to his retreating troops, "Look at Jackson; he stands like a stone wall." That night Gen. Bee died, and Jackson was ever known afterward as "Stonewall Jackson."

Yes, the Union army was beaten, and their retreat developed into a disastrous rout, although they were not pursued by the Confederates.

While there was great rejoicing all over the South on account of this splendid victory gained by our raw recruits, there was no noisy demonstrations. Crowds thronged the streets, but no bonfires lit up the darkness of the night. No cannon thundered out salutes. The church steeples were silent, except when in solemn tone they called the people to prayer.

The next day the Confederate Congress met and passed the following resolutions:

We recognize the hand of the most high God, the King of Kings and Lord of Lords, in the glorious victory with which he has crowned our armies at Manassas, and that the people of these Confederate States are invited by appropriate services on the ensuing Sabbath to offer up their united thanksgiving and prayers for this mighty deliverance.

The losses in men were as follows: Union army, 3000; Confederates, 2000. The latter captured 27 cannon, 1500 prisoners, an immense quantity of small arms, ammunition, stores, etc.

I promptly laid aside my flint-lock musket and took a Springfield rifle.

I am often amused as I remember some of the thoughts that passed through my mind, and some of the things I did on this momentous occasion. For instance, we were ordered to "sleep on our arms" the night whose dawn was to usher in the battle. I had heard a good deal about soldiers obeying orders. I thought of "*the boy who stood on the burning deck*," so when I laid down that night with old Mother Earth for a bed, I found myself stretched out at full length on top of my musket. It was a little rough, but the mere thought of being a soldier and "sleeping on my arms" on the eve of battle made my bed feel as soft as a bed of roses. And then the gun! It was an old flint-lock musket, minus the flint, and no powder or ball. But I was at least a soldier and had a gun, and would surely see the battle and could write home all about it. A soldier seldom ever thinks that he will be among the slain; he may be wounded, or taken prisoner, but it is always the other fellow that is going to be killed.

CHAPTER 3

From Bull Run to Seven Pines (Continued)

You have called us and we're coming, by Richmond's bloody tide
To lay us down, for freedom's sake, our brothers' bones beside.

The several battles around Richmond in the spring of 1862, *viz.*, Seven Pines, Mechanicsville, Beaver Dam, Malvern Hill, Gaines' Mill, I have grouped under the head of Seven Pines.

The fall and winter months following the battle of Bull Run were spent for the most part by both sides in recruiting their armies and getting ready for a desperate struggle, which would inevitably come when spring arrived the following year.

There were occasional raids and skirmishes, but no decisive battles were fought until the following spring, except the battle of Ball's Bluff, near Leesburg, in which battle the Eighth Virginia played a conspicuous part. One of my brothers was in this battle, and several of my schoolmates were killed and wounded.

Johnston's army a few days after the battle had increased to 40,000. He moved forward and occupied a position near Centerville, and there he wintered. Jackson, however, was detached and sent back to Winchester to guard the valley, and became commander-in-chief of that section. The forces that came down from Leesburg returned to their old position.

During the winter the soldiers were granted frequent furloughs, the militia was disbanded, and I went back home.

But when the birds began heralding the coming of spring

there was a call from the Confederate Government not only for the return of all enlisted men to their commands, but for every able-bodied white male citizen between the ages of eighteen and forty-five to enlist.

I started out from Middleburg with Edwin Bailey and several Marylanders, the latter having crossed the Potomac for the purpose of joining the Confederate army. Bailey was already a member of the Eighth Virginia Infantry, and was at home on furlough.

My destination was the Sixth Virginia Cavalry, which was then with Stonewall Jackson in the valley of Virginia. This regiment was in Robinson's brigade, Fitzhugh Lee's division, the whole cavalry force of the army of Northern Virginia being commanded by Gen. J.E.B. Stuart. I was on horseback; the others on foot.

It reminded me of the resurrection morn, except the trooping thousands were coming from the top of the ground and not from under it. From hamlet and villa, from the lordly mansion and mountain shack, from across the Potomac, the boys and young men of the South were coming in answer to the call. The Government at Washington had called for half a million; the Government at Richmond had called for every able-bodied son from eighteen to forty-five, and they were coming.

The nearest point at which I could reach the Confederate line was Harrisonburg, Va. All the district between my home and Harrisonburg, and on the line stretching from there south to the James river, and north into West Virginia, had been abandoned to the enemy. Hence, it was necessary for us to move with great caution, to avoid being intercepted by the bluecoats. The little caravan moved up the pike that runs from Alexandria across the Blue Ridge into the valley by the way of Upperville and Paris. When we reached the mountain at Paris we moved along its foot, travelling mostly by night and resting by day, hiding ourselves in the heavy timber that stretched along the slopes of the mountain.

We had no trouble procuring food from the little farm houses that we passed. Occasionally we employed a guide, whom we paid. These guides took great pains to magnify the danger that surrounded us, and told us of the narrow escapes of other caravans that had preceded us. This was done in order to draw as large a fee from us as possible. The distance to Harrisonburg was about 100 miles. We finally reached our destination.

During the winter and early spring the North had raised a very large army, splendidly equipped, and placed under the command of Gen. George B. McClellan. This army was taken mostly by boat to a point on the James River, from which point it took up a line of march toward Richmond. McClellan's army was the largest and best equipped that had ever trod American soil.

McClellan was the idol of the North, and there was very little doubt in the minds of the Northern people that when he met the Confederate forces defending Richmond the Capital of the Confederacy would be captured, and the army defending it destroyed or captured.

The Confederate forces gradually fell back before McClellan's army as it advanced along the James River, until the invaders could see the spires of the Confederate Capitol.

Of course, this move of McClellan's having made Johnston's position at Centerville untenable, he withdrew his army and marched to Richmond, so as to confront McClellan on his arrival.

The day finally arrived when McClellan was to make the attack that was to result in the overthrow of the Confederacy.

While this was going on, Gen. Joseph E. Johnston (who commanded the Confederate forces) was busy strengthening his position and preparing his army for the coming struggle.

Jackson had in the meantime distinguished himself in the valley by routing three armies, each larger than his own, that had been sent out to capture him. Having defeated these armies, he fell back beyond Harrisonburg, and then quietly slipped out of the valley, crossed the Blue Ridge Mountains, and made a rapid march toward Richmond.

Instead of uniting his forces with those of Johnston, he moved his army to a point toward McClellan's rear, and at once began an attack which, combined with Johnston's attack in the front, resulted in a disastrous retreat of the Northern army.

Johnston was severely wounded during the first days of the battle, which lasted seven days, and Gen. Robert E. Lee assumed command of the army now known as the army of Northern Virginia, and held the position to the end of the war. Lee also became commander-in-chief of all the Confederate armies.

When McClellan fully realized that it was Jackson's army from the valley that "was goring his side like the horns of an angry bull," it is said that the scene at his headquarters was intensely dramatic. From information received from Washington, McClellan had every reason to believe that Jackson and his entire army were either prisoners or cooped up somewhere in the valley north of Harrisonburg, but as the sound of Jackson's guns grew louder and nearer, and couriers with panting steeds came dashing in confirming the truth, he was forced to believe that the noise was Jackson's "cannon's opening roar." "Then there was hurrying to and fro and mounting in hot haste." Never did human brain work quicker than did McClellan's when he realized his position. Who but a Napoleon could provide so quickly for such an emergency? The masterly manner in which McClellan changed his base and saved his army, with three such strategists as Jackson, Lee and Johnston to reckon with, showed military skill of the highest order.

Someone in conversation with Gen. Lee after the war asked who was the greatest soldier on the side of the North. Lee replied, "McClellan, by all odds." The fact is, the Government at Washington never gave McClellan a fair chance. Gen. Lee came to Richmond from West Virginia, where his campaign had been a failure, and was elevated at once to the most important post in the Confederate army, while McClellan was humiliated by being relieved of his command just at a time when he was prepared by experience to put into use his great talent. History is bound to record him a place among the famous generals.

The battle lasted seven full days. The Confederate victory was complete. Millions of dollars' worth of supplies were captured or destroyed, and McClellan was compelled to beat a hasty retreat to Washington to defend the city.

The spoils of this battle that fell into the hands of the Confederates were 10,000 prisoners, 35,000 rifles, 55 cannon, ammunition, provision stores of every kind, almost beyond computation. The losses of the two armies in killed and wounded were nearly equal—about 10,000 each.

Some idea can be formed of the captured stores when it is remembered that to provide for an army such as McClellan's, 600 tons of ammunition, food, forage and medical supplies had to be forwarded from Washington every day. If he kept a thirty days' supply on hand, we have the enormous sum of 18,000 tons that either fell into the hands of the Confederates or was destroyed.

When I reached Harrisonburg I found the Sixth Virginia Cavalry had left the valley with Jackson's army. I followed as rapidly as possible, and met the regiment at Gordonsville, with Jackson's army, coming back from the battle and hurrying on toward Manassas to attack Pope, who had gathered an army there to protect Washington while McClellan was besieging Richmond. I joined Company A of the Sixth Virginia Cavalry and felt that I was a full-fledged cavalryman and was ready to take part in anything that the regiment was called upon to do.

CHAPTER 4

From Seven Pines to Antietam

On that pleasant morn of early fall,
When Lee marched over the mountain wall.

Over the mountains, winding down,
Horse and foot into Frederick town.

A part of Pope's army, under Banks, had been pushed forward as far as Cedar Run, about half way between Manassas and
Gordonsville. Jackson met this force and scattered it like chaff,
and then moved rapidly toward Manassas. He did not move in a
straight line, but made a detour to the left, and by rapid marches
placed his army in the rear of Pope at Manassas.

One day the army covered forty miles. Riding along the
dusty highway, Jackson noticed a sore-foot, barefoot infantry-
man, limping along, trying to keep up with his command. Coming up to him, he dismounted and told the soldier to mount his
horse, while he trudged along by his side. The next day the same
soldier was found among the dead, with his face turned up to
the sun, having given his life for the man who gave him a lift. It
was this lift that had cost him his life; but for it, he would have
been among the stragglers, too late for the battle.

My command, during the march, got in frequent touch with
the enemy, and at one point, namely, Catletts Station, on the Orange and Alexandria Railroad, came very near capturing Gen.
Pope himself. We got into his camp at night and into his tent,
and took his boots and spurs, and papers that gave Jackson some

valuable information.

As soon as Gen. Lee was satisfied that McClellan was well on his way toward Washington, he put his whole army in motion and moved rapidly to join Jackson, who would sorely need him in his attack upon Pope at Manassas; in fact, Jackson had halted after the battle of Cedar Run for a day or two to allow Gen. Lee to come up.

An event occurred during this battle around Richmond that brought sorrow to my home. My brother Howard was slightly wounded in the arm, taken to the hospital at Richmond, and died in a few days of a malignant fever, and was buried somewhere among the unknown dead around Richmond. The family made several attempts to locate his grave, but were unsuccessful.

> *On fame's eternal camping ground,*
> *His silent tent is spread;*
> *While glory guards with solemn round*
> *The bivouac of the dead.*

His picture on the following page is from an old daguerreotype, taken just before entering the Confederate service.

This move of Jackson's to the rear of Pope at Manassas enabled him to capture many carloads of supplies and munitions of war, greatly assisting the armies of Lee and Jackson in their undertaking. A goodly portion of McClellan's army had embarked at Occoquan and marched across to the assistance of Pope. Notwithstanding this fact, the combined armies of Lee and Jackson were more than a match for Pope, and he was defeated and his army routed, leaving over 9000 of his dead and wounded on the field. His entire loss, as given by the *New Standard Encyclopaedia*, which included prisoners, was 20,000, while the Confederates', by the same authority, is placed at 12,000.

There fell into the hands of the Confederates 7000 prisoners, 30 cannon, 20,000 rifles. The captured stores, including two miles of loaded cars on the track, was enormous, much of which the Confederates had to burn.

Robert Howard Hopkins.

This is called the Second Battle of Manassas to distinguish it from the first battle fought on the same ground, and called by the North the Battle of Bull Run, but by the South as the First Battle of Manassas.

Pope lost no time in getting behind his intrenchments at Washington. My command took part in the battle, and made a charge just as the sun was dropping behind the horizon. Lee did not follow Pope toward Washington, but moved in a straight line toward the Upper Potomac, leaving Washington to his right.

At this time my company was detached from the Sixth Regiment and made a bodyguard to Gen. Lee. We kept close to his person both night and day.

Part of the time Gen. Lee rode in an ambulance with both hands bandaged, his horse, "Traveller," having fallen over a log and crippled Lee's hands. This gave me a good opportunity of seeing the great soldier at close range.

I remember one afternoon, when toward sunset the army having gone into camp for the night, Gen. Lee's headquarters being established in a little farmhouse near Chantilla, I think in Loudoun county, the General went out with one of his staff officers for a walk into an apple orchard. They were gone perhaps an hour. While they were gone a guard had been set around the cottage with instructions to let none pass without an order from Gen. Lee.

When Gen. Lee returned with his aid by his side, he was halted by Frank Peak (a member of my company, now living in Alexandria, Va.). They both halted, and Peak said to them, "My instructions are to let none pass without an order from Gen. Lee." Gen. Lee turned to his aid and said, "Stop, the sentinel has halted us." The officer (I think it was Col. Marshall, who afterward lived in Baltimore, and died there not long ago) stepped forward and said, "This is Gen. Lee himself, who gives all orders." Peak saluted them, and they passed on.

Before day the next morning the army was in motion toward Maryland, Gen. Lee still riding in the ambulance, very much, no doubt, to the chagrin of "Traveler," who was led by a soldier, just behind the ambulance.

Owing to the hard-fought battles around Richmond, Cedar Run and Manassas (which followed each other in rapid succession), and the long, weary marches through the hot July days, often far into the night, many of Lee's soldiers, who were footsore and broken down, straggled from the ranks, being unable to keep up with the stronger men. So great was the number that it was said that half his army were straggling along the roads and through the fields, subsisting as they could on fruits and berries, and whatever food they could get from farmhouses.

As the army crossed the Potomac (four miles east of Leesburg) Gen. Lee had to make some provision for the stragglers. It would not do to let them follow the army into the enemy's country, because they would all be captured. He concluded to abandon his bodyguard and leave it at the river, with instructions to turn the stragglers and tell them to move toward Winchester, beyond the Shenandoah. This was the point, no doubt, that Gen. Lee had fixed as the place to which he would bring his army when his Maryland campaign was over.

It was with much regret that we had to give up our post of honour as guard to the head of the army to take charge of sorefooted stragglers. But a soldier's duty is to obey orders.

The army crossed the river into Maryland, and we were kept busy for a week sending the stragglers toward Winchester.

Some bore wounds received in the battles mentioned, and their bandages in many cases still showed the dried blood as evidence that they had not always been stragglers. Some were sick, and some too lame to walk, and it became necessary for us to go out among the farmers and procure wagons to haul the disabled. In doing so, it was my duty to call on an old Quaker family by the name of Janney, near Goose Creek meeting-house, Loudoun county, and get his four-horse wagon and order it to Leesburg. This I did in good soldier style, not appreciating the old adage that *Chickens come home to roost.*

After seeing the wagon on the road, accompanied by friend Janney, who rode on horseback (the wagon being driven by his hired man), I went to other farms, doing the same thing. And thus the lame, sick and sore-footed and the rag-and-tag were pushed on, shoved on and hauled on toward Winchester.

Some years after this I had occasion to visit the same spot, in company with a young lady.

It was the Friends' quarterly meeting time at Goose Creek. We attended the services, and, of course, were invited out to dinner. It fell to our lot to dine at the home of friend Janney, from whom I had taken the wagon. I did not recognize the house or the family until I was painfully reminded of it in the following manner:

We were seated at a long table in the dining-room (I think there were at least twenty at the table), and several young ladies were acting as waitresses. I was quite bashful in those days, but was getting along very nicely, until one of the young waitresses, perhaps with no intention of embarrassing me, focusing her mild blue eyes upon mine, said, "I think I recognize thee as one of the soldiers who took our wagon and team for the use of Lee's army, *en route* for Maryland."

I did not look up, but felt that twice twenty eyes were centred on me. I cannot recall what I said, but I am sure I pleaded guilty; besides, I felt that all the blood in my body had gone to my face, and that every drop was crying out, "Yes, he's the very fellow." It spoiled my dinner, but they all seemed to think it was a good joke on me.

Quakers, it must be remembered, were not as a rule in sympathy with the secession movement, which greatly intensified the discomfort of my position. My young friend, however, although a member of that society, never deserted me, and sometime afterward became more to me than a friend; she has been faithful ever since, and is now sitting by me as I write these lines.

Now I must go back to war scenes.

I cannot remember, of course, just the day, but while we were busy gathering up these stragglers we could distinctly hear the booming of the guns that told us the two armies had met and that there was heavy fighting on Maryland soil.

The first sounds came from toward Harper's Ferry, and we soon afterward learned the result.

Jackson had been detached from the main army, had surrounded and captured Harper's Ferry, taking 13,000 prisoners and many army supplies. Among the prisoners was A.W. Green of New York, who afterward became pastor of my church, St. John's, corner Madison avenue and Laurens street, Baltimore, Md.

Mr. Green says that when the prisoners were all lined up, Jackson rode along their front and tried to comfort them as best he could. He said, "Men, this is the fate of war; it is you today, it may be us tomorrow." After paroling his prisoners, Jackson hurried to rejoin Lee, who was being hotly pressed by McClellan at Antietam. Lee's united forces at this time could not have numbered over 40,000 men, while McClellan, who was still in command of the Union army, had a force of over 100,000.

McClellan made the attack, was repulsed with terrible loss, but the North claimed the victory, because Lee retired during the second night after the battle and re-crossed the Potomac, falling back to Winchester, where he was reinforced by the stragglers who had been gathering there for two weeks or more.

This series of battles, beginning with Richmond in the spring and ending at Antietam in the early fall, had so exhausted the armies that both sides were glad to take a rest. They had been marching and fighting from early spring all through the summer, and were thoroughly exhausted.

LEE'S ARMY IN A TRAP.

We have all heard of the famous lost dispatch that was picked up in the streets of Frederick, Md., after the place had been evacuated by the Confederates. It was called *Special Order No. 191*. A copy of this order was sent by Gen. Lee to each of his generals. The one intended for Gen. A.P. Hill never reached him. It was dropped by a courier and fell into the hands of Gen. McClellan. This telltale slip of paper that might have ended the war was found wrapped around two cigars. It read as follows:

Headquarters Army of Northern Virginia,
near Frederick, Md.

September 9, 1862.

Special Orders, No. 191.

The army will resume its march tomorrow, taking the Hagerstown road. General Jackson's command will form the advance, and, after passing Middletown, with such portion as he may select, take the route toward Sharpsburg, cross the Potomac at the most convenient point, and, by Friday night, take possession of the Baltimore & Ohio Railroad, capture such of the enemy as may be at Martinsburg, and intercept such as may attempt to escape from Harper's Ferry.

General Longstreet's command will pursue the same road as far as Boonsborough, where it will halt with the reserve, supply and baggage trains of the army.

General McLaws, with his own division and that of General R. H. Anderson, will follow General Longstreet. On reaching Middletown he will take the route to Harper's Ferry, and by Friday morning possess himself of the Maryland Heights and endeavour to capture the enemy at Harper's Ferry and vicinity.

General Walker, with his division, after accomplishing the object in which he is now engaged, will cross the Potomac at Cheek's Ford, ascend its right bank to Lovettsville, take possession of Loudoun Heights, if practicable, by Friday morning. Key's Ford on his left, and the road between the end of the mountain and the Potomac on his right. He will, as far as practicable, co-operate with General McLaws and General Jackson in intercepting the retreat of the enemy.

General D.H. Hill's division will form the rear guard of the army, pursuing the road taken by the main body. The reserve artillery, ordnance, supply-trains, etc., will precede General Hill.

General Stuart will detach a squadron of cavalry to accompany the commands of Generals Longstreet, Jackson and McLaws, and with the main body of the cavalry will cover the route of the army and bring up all stragglers that may have been left behind.

The commands of Generals Jackson, McLaws and Walker, after accomplishing the objects for which they have been detached, will join the main body of the army at Boonsborough or Hagerstown.

Each regiment on the march will habitually carry its axes in the regimental ordnance wagons for use of the men at their encampments to procure wood, etc.

By command of General R.E. Lee.

With this document in his hands and with Lee's army divided as it was McClellan felt that his hour had come. He sent the following dispatch to President Lincoln:

> . . . . . I have all the plans of the rebels, and will catch them in their own trap. . . . . .General Lee's order to his army accidentally came into my hands this evening, and discloses his plan of campaign."

The destruction of Lee's army at this time would certainly have ended hostilities. Gen. Longstreet was opposed to the movement against Harper's Ferry. He said it was fraught with too much danger. It was rendered much more so when McClellan came into possession of Lee's plans. The exact number of prisoners captured at Harper's Ferry and in its environments were 12,520, together with 73 cannon, 13,000 rifles, several hundred wagons and large quantities of provisions and other army stores.

CHAPTER 5

From Antietam to Chancellorsville

Two armies covered hill and plain,
Where Rappahannock's waters
Ran deeply crimsoned with the stain
Of battle's recent slaughters.

After resting a while at Winchester Lee's army began its march leisurely back toward Richmond, and took up a position near Fredericksburg, a point about half way between Washington and Richmond.

McClellan was relieved of his command, and Gen. Burnside took his place and gathered a large army in front of Fredericksburg on the Rappahannock River.

About the middle of December Burnside crossed the river at Fredericksburg by means of pontoon bridges and attacked Lee and Jackson just outside of the town of Fredericksburg.

A severe battle was fought, and Burnside was defeated with terrible loss. He re-crossed the river and wept when he contemplated the awful slaughter that had been made in his army. This ended the campaign of 1862. It is said that more soldiers fell in this battle in four hours than were killed in the entire Boer War. The historian has placed Burnside's losses at 12,311; Lee's at 5409.

Both armies went into winter quarters, and there was no general battle until the next spring, but frequent skirmishes between bodies of cavalry on both sides as they marched to and fro protecting their respective encampments.

From Harper's Ferry to Staunton, Va., stretches a part of the Blue Ridge Mountains that played a conspicuous part in the war.

The mountain is impassable for armies except through the gaps that occur every twenty to thirty miles. These gaps were always closely guarded by the Confederates, and through them the armies frequently marched and counter-marched as occasion required.

If Jackson needed reinforcements in the valley, they were sent to him through one of these gaps; and on the other hand, if the armies defending Richmond needed reinforcements, it was Jackson's custom to give the enemy a stinging blow and send him in full retreat down the valley toward Washington, then cross through one of these gaps with a portion of his army and reinforce the armies defending Richmond.

When the armies fell back from Winchester my company of cavalry was left to guard the Bluemount gap, then called Snickersville. A little later the gap was abandoned, and we were ordered to Ashby's gap, farther up the valley, where we encamped near the little town of Paris, at the foot of the mountain, and put out our pickets on the east side of the mountain below Upperville on the pike that leads through Middleburg and on to Alexandria, Va., just under the shadow of the capital of the Northern nation, I will call it.

One day our pickets reported "the enemy's cavalry advancing up the pike toward Upperville." Our captain (Bruce Gibson) ordered the bugle sounded, and 90 to 100 men were soon in the saddle and on the march to meet the enemy.

It was four miles to Upperville, and as we approached the town we could distinctly see the enemy's cavalry filling the streets.

We halted at a point just opposite the home of our captain (where the family were on the porch watching the movements of both sides). Many of the men of the company lived in that neighbourhood. It was eight miles from my home, hence this was no place to show the "white feather."

I was riding a fiery young mare. She was never satisfied unless she was a little ahead. She had a mouth that no bit could hold.

The captain ordered us to move forward, and as we approached the town, four abreast, our speed was increased to a trot, then to a gallop.

To the best of my recollection my position was about the middle of the command, but in spite of my tugging at the bit, my young steed carried me up to the front, and when we got close enough to the enemy to see the whites of their eyes, I was a little closer to them than I wanted to be, and I'll frankly confess it wasn't bravery that put me there. We were close enough to discover that we were running into a whole regiment of Union cavalry, and if we had continued, it would have meant annihilation.

The captain ordered right about, retreat! At this point to get those 100 horses turned around in that street and get out of the reach of 1000 guns in the hands of 1000 Bluecoats, was a knotty problem. If the enemy had charged us just at this time, our destruction would have been just as complete as it would have been if we had gone ahead; but they hesitated. Perhaps they were afraid of running into a trap.

I ran my horse up against a pump, and finally got turned around, and was soon leaving my comrades behind me, for she was fleet of foot. But all at once I felt my steed going down under me. I thought that she was shot, but did not have much time to think about it, for I was soon for a few minutes unconscious. My horse had tripped and fallen, and, of course, I could not keep the saddle, going at a speed like that. The horse just behind leaped over me, horse and all (so the rider afterward told me). When I came to myself I was standing in the middle of the road with a crowd of Yankees around me, among them the colonel of the regiment. I was holding in my hand the handle of my pistol, the barrel of which had been broken off by the fall. When called upon to surrender my arms I meekly handed up this handle, scarcely knowing what I was doing. One of the Yankees said, "I don't want that, I want your arms." My arms consisted of a sabre, a short cavalry gun and another pistol, that remained in its holder.

With some assistance I unbuckled my belt and gave up my arms. The colonel asked me if I was hurt, and some other questions which I cannot now recall.

His own horse had been down on its knees, which were badly skinned. He dismounted and mounted another horse that had been brought to him, and told me I could have the use of his horse. I mounted with some difficulty, and was taken to the rear. There was very little firing; only one man was killed and one horse on our side.

My horse, they afterward told me, passed through the command and did not stop until she got to Paris, four miles beyond.

The Yankees remained only a short time, when they began their retreat down the pike with one lone prisoner, myself. On the way they picked up three or four citizens, which gave me some company.

It was quite dark when we reached Middleburg, and the command halted in the town for an hour, during which time I sat on my horse just in front of the house now occupied by Edwin LeRoy Broun.

I could see the lights in the windows and see the family moving about, among them my sister. I made no effort to make myself known. After an hour's wait the command moved down the pike toward Washington, arriving at Fairfax Courthouse about midnight, where they went into camp. The next morning some 15 or 20 prisoners were brought in and put in an old log schoolhouse. We remained there all that day, and the next day the citizens were released, and the soldier prisoners (about a dozen) were started for Washington under a guard of four cavalrymen. We were taken to the old capitol at Washington and put in one of the rooms. I suppose there were several hundred prisoners there at the time. We remained about a month, when we were exchanged. We were taken to Richmond by boat and turned over to the authorities there, and our Government released a similar number of Union prisoners who returned on the same boat that brought us to Richmond. I took the train at Richmond, rode to Gordonsville, and footed it from there home, a distance of about 150 miles.

I found my horse awaiting me, and after a few days rest, I mounted and rejoined my command at the little town of Paris, Fauquier county, where I had left them for a visit to Washington as a guest of the United States Government.

As the winter came on the Confederates drew in their outposts, and likewise the enemy. This left the whole eastern part of Virginia free from the depredations of either army, except now and then a raid from one side on the other.

My regiment was at camp in the woods near Harrisonburg, while Jackson's main army was with Lee, south of Fredericksburg. Jackson spent much time during the winter in religious work among his soldiers. "My ambition," he said, "is to command a converted army." He himself was one of the most devout men in the army, and seemed to be always in communion with his God.

The winter was a hard one, and both armies kept pretty well within their winter quarters.

We had no tents, but took fence rails, and putting one end on a pole fastened to two trees, and the other on the ground, and covering the rails with leaves and fastening up each end, leaving the front open, then building a big fire just in front, we had a very comfortable place to sleep. We sat on logs around the fire during the day and far into the night telling stories and entertaining ourselves in various ways. At night we crept under the roof of our shed, which was about a foot deep in leaves, and slept as comfortably as any farmer's hogs would do under similar circumstances.

About the first of January my company was again detached from the regiment and sent to Orkney Springs, just at the foot of North mountain, west of Strasburg.

Our duty was to keep a dozen men on the opposite side of the mountain scouting and doing picket duty. It was our custom to relieve the men once a week by sending over another detachment and relieving those on duty.

While at Orkney Springs we occupied cottages that were intended for the summer guests prior to the breaking out of hostilities. But after remaining in the cottages some time, the health of the command was so poor that we were compelled to go back to the woods. In a short time the sickness disappeared from the camp, showing that the best place for a soldier is out in the open.

Shortly after this word came that the enemy was advancing up the valley turnpike, and the whole regiment was ordered down to meet them, our company in advance.

It was March. The day was a stormy one. It snowed and rained alternately all day long, far into the night.

When we left camp I was suffering with rheumatism in my hip, so that I had to use a stump to mount my horse, for I was determined to go with the regiment. Soldiers lying in camp idle soon get restless, and even cowards will hail with delight a chance to have a brush with the enemy.

So notwithstanding the weather and physical ailments of some of the men, all went out of camp that morning bright and happy.

We marched all day until long after dark, and then discovered it was a false alarm. The Yankees were snug in their tents, many miles away.

We went into camp in the woods. I remember that I was wet to the skin, and I can see myself now sitting on a log pulling off first one long-legged boot, then the other, and pouring the water out.

But before this, fires had sprung up all over the woods. In spite of the fact that everything was drenched and water was dripping from every twig, in an incredibly short time the whole woods were brilliantly illuminated by burning camp-fires.

We got out our bacon and crackers and enjoyed a supper that no *habitué* of a Delmonico could have relished more. The bacon (not sugar-cured) was stuck on a stick and roasted before the fire, while the grease was allowed to fall on the cracker on a chip below.

The Delmonico man might boast of a higher grade of food and better cooking, but the soldier wins on the appetite.

After supper we stood around the camp-fires drying the outside of our clothes, telling stories and smoking. Then we prepared for bed.

The men in the companies are always divided into messes; the average number of men in each was usually about six. The messes were like so many families that lived together, slept together and ate together, and stood by each other in all emergencies. There was no rule regulating the messes. The men simply came together by common consent. *Birds of a feather flock together.*

In winter one bed was made for the whole mess. It consisted of laying down rubber cloths on the ground and covering them with a blanket, and another and another, as occasion required, and if the weather was foul, on top of that other rubber cloths. Our saddles covered with our coats were our pillows. The two end men had logs of wood to protect them. Only our coats and boots were removed.

On a cold winter night, no millionaire on his bed of down ever slept sweeter than a soldier on a bed like this.

In the summer each soldier had a separate bed. If it was raining, he made his bed on top of two fence rails, if he could not find a better place. If the weather was good, old Mother Earth was all the soldier wanted.

As this was a cold, stormy night, of course we all bunked together. My, what a nice, soft, sweaty time we had! The next morning all traces of my rheumatism had disappeared, and I felt as spry as a young kitten.

As the day advanced the clouds rolled by, the sun came out bright and smiling, and the command marched back to the old camp-ground, near Harrisonburg.

With every regiment there is a Company Q. Company Q is composed of lame ducks, cowards, shirkers, dead-beats, generally, and also a large sprinkling of good soldiers, who, for some reason or other, are not fit for duty. Sometimes this company is quite large. It depends upon the weather, the closeness of the enemy, and the duties that are being exacted. Bad weather will drive in all rheumatics; the coming battle will drive in the cowards; hard marching and picket duty will bring in the lazy. But then, as I have just said, there were some good soldiers among them—the slightly wounded or those suffering from any disability. Taking them altogether, Company Q resembled Mother Goose's beggars that came to town; *some in rags, some in tags, and some in velvet gowns.* Company Q was always the butt of the joker.

A short time after the regiment had returned from its fruitless march down the pike, the four regiments composing the brigade under Gen. William E. Jones were ordered to break camp and move across the mountains into the enemy's country in West Virginia.

At that time I was almost blind with inflamed eyes. They looked like two clots of blood. Of course, I did not go with the command, but was forced to join Company Q. As well as I remember, the company numbered at that time over 100 men, among them two or three officers.

As the regiment expected to be absent for over a month and to return crowned with laurels, Company Q conceived the idea of doing something that would put them on an equal footing with their comrades when they returned from this expedition.

A company was formed of about 100 men, which were soon on the march down the valley pike. My eyes had so improved that I could join the company.

The enemy was encamped near Winchester, perhaps 75 miles away. Our destination was this camp. We were to march down the valley, make a night attack and come back with all the plunder we could carry off or drive off. Every fellow expected to bring back at least one extra horse.

We reached the west branch of the Shenandoah, near Strasburg, and went into camp for the night, having first put out pickets at the various fords up and down the river.

The enemy's camp was supposed to be ten miles beyond. We

intended to remain at this camp until the next evening about dusk, and then start for the enemy, timing ourselves to reach their camp about midnight.

The next morning about 9 o'clock we came down from our camp into the open field to graze our horses. We had taken the bits out of their mouths and were lying around loose, while the horses cropped the grass, when all at once someone shouted "Yankees." Sure enough, there they were, a whole regiment of Union cavalrymen. They had crossed the river some distance below our pickets and had placed themselves directly in our rear, cutting off our retreat. We soon had our horses bridled, and mounting, made for the river. The commander sent me down the river to call in the pickets, but I did not go far until I met them coming in. They had heard the firing. We had a desperate race to join the fleeing company, but did so, narrowly escaping capture.

There was a small body of woods on the banks of the river, where we found shelter for the moment. We were entirely cut off from the fords, and there was no way of crossing the river but to swim. The banks were steep on each side, so it looked as if that would be the last of poor Company Q. We dismounted, got behind the trees, and were ready to give our tormentors a warm reception, but Providence seemed to smile on us. Someone discovered a little stream running into the river. We followed that down into the river, and the whole command swam across and climbed the banks on the other side, except one man (Milton Robinson) and myself.

Our horses refused to swim. They behaved so ugly that we had to abandon them. Mine was the same "jade" that had dumped me on the Yankees a few months before. Now I had a chance to reciprocate. I tied her to a little sapling at the edge of the river, and Robinson and I hid in the bushes close by the banks. The Yankees came down and took our horses, and after searching around for some time, vacated the premises, much to our gratification.

The loss of our horses grieved us very much, but such is the life of a soldier.

The company in crossing the river were in the enemy's country, and were liable to be surrounded and captured at any time, but they made their escape in some way, and lost no time in getting back to camp, many miles away.

Robinson and I, of course, had to foot it, but in course of time we also landed in camp, much to the surprise of our comrades, who thought the enemy had us. Thus terminated ingloriously the well-planned expedition of Company Q.

In about ten days the brigade came back from the West Virginia expedition, and Company Q received the Sixth Regiment with open arms. Just what the expedition accomplished I am not able to say, but there is one little incident connected with it that has lingered lovingly in my memory to this day.

Every mess had in it a forager; that is, one skilled in the art of picking up delicacies. At least we called them such, as this term was applied to anything edible above hardtack and salt pork. We had such a one in our mess, and he was hard to beat. His name was Fauntleroy Neal. He was a close friend of mine. We called him Faunt.

Whenever he went on an expedition he always came back loaded. As he was with the brigade in West Virginia, we knew that when he returned (if he did return) he would bring back something good, and he did. I cannot remember all the things he had strapped to his saddle, but one thing looms up before my mind now as big as a Baltimore skyscraper. It was about half a bushel of genuine grain coffee, unroasted. There was also sugar to sweeten it. Grains of coffee in the South during the Civil War were as scarce as grains of gold, and when toasting time came and the lid was lifted to stir the coffee, it is said that the aroma from it spread through the trees and over the fields for many miles around. I forgot the long, weary march on foot back up the valley, forgot the loss of my horse, and really felt as if I had been fully compensated for any inconvenience that had come to me from the ill-starred tramp of Company Q.

But spring had fully come, the roads were dry, and the time

for action was here.

Hooker, at the head of 120,000 Northern soldiers, was again crossing the Rappahannock, near Fredericksburg, to lock horns with Lee and Jackson.

Hooker had superseded Burnside in command of the Union army. They called him "fighting Joe."

Hooker handled his army the first two or three days with consummate skill, and at one stage of his manoeuvres he felt confident that he had outgeneralled Lee and Jackson. He believed they were in full retreat, and so informed the Washington Government. But he was doomed to a terrible disappointment. What Hooker took to be a retreat of the Confederates was simply a change of front, which was followed up by Jackson executing another one of his bold flank movements, the most brilliant of his brief career, the result of which was Hooker's defeat. The entire Union army was thrown into such confusion that it was compelled to retreat across the river, after sustaining heavy losses in killed and wounded.

The *New Standard Encyclopaedia* gives Hooker's army as 130,000; Lee's, 60,000. Hooker's losses, 18,000; Lee's, 13,000.

Perhaps no general on either side during the entire war felt more keenly his defeat than did Hooker on this occasion. For awhile everything seemed to be going his way, when suddenly the tide turned, and he saw his vast army in a most critical situation, and apparently at the mercy of his opponent.

History tells the whole story in better language than I can. It calls it the *Battle of Chancellorsville.*

Carl Schurz, one of the generals in Hooker's army, says that never did Gen. Lee's qualities as a soldier shine as brilliantly as they did in this battle. To quote his own language,

> We had 120,000 men, Lee 60,000. Yet Lee handled his forces so skilfully that whenever he attacked he did it with a superior force, and in this way he overwhelmed our army and compelled its retreat, after suffering terrible losses not only in dead and wounded, but in prisoners.

But the Confederates also suffered a tremendous loss at Chancellorsville. Just at the moment when he was about to gather the fruit of his victory, which might have resulted in the surrender of Hooker's army, or the greater portion of it, Stonewall Jackson was fired on by his own men, mortally wounded, and died a few days afterwards.

The following account of the wounding of Jackson, as related by an eye-witness, will be of interest to the reader:

It was 9 o'clock at night. There was a lull in the battle, and Jackson's line had become somewhat disorganized by the men gathering in groups and discussing their brilliant victory. Jackson, noticing the confusion, rode up and down the line, saying, "Men, get into line, get into line; I need your help for a time. This disorder must be corrected."

He had just received information that a large body of fresh troops from the Union army was advancing to retake an important position that it had lost. Jackson had gone 100 yards in front of his own line to get a better view of the enemy's position. The only light that he had to guide him was that furnished by the moon.

He was attended by half a dozen orderlies and several of his staff officers, when he was suddenly surprised by a volley of musketry in his front. The bullets began whistling about them, and struck several horses. This was the advance guard of the Federal lines. Jackson, seeing the danger, turned and rode rapidly back toward his own line. As he approached, the Confederate troops, mistaking them for the enemy's cavalry, stooped and delivered a deadly fire. So sudden was this volley, and so near at hand, that every horse which was not shot down recoiled from it in panic and turned to rush back, bearing his rider toward the approaching enemy.

Several fell dead on the spot, and more were wounded, among them Gen. Jackson. His right hand was penetrated by a ball, his left was lacerated by another, and the same arm was broken a little below the shoulder by a third ball, which not only crushed the bone, but severed the main artery. His horse dashed, panic-stricken, toward the enemy, carrying him beneath the boughs of the trees, which inflicted several blows, lacerated his face, and almost dragged him from the saddle. His bridle hand was now powerless, but seizing the rein with his right hand, notwithstanding its wound, he arrested his horse and brought the animal back toward his own line.

He was followed by his faithful attendants. The firing of the Confederates had now been arrested by some of the officers, who realized their mistake, but the wounded and frantic horses were rushing without riders through the woods, where the ground was strewn with the dead and dying. Here Gen. Jackson drew up his horse and sat for an instant, gazing toward his own line, as if in astonishment at their cruel mistake, and in doubt whether he should again venture to approach them. He said to one of his staff, "I believe my arm is broken," and requested him to assist him from his horse and examine whether the wounds were bleeding dangerously.

Before he could dismount he sank fainting into their arms, so completely prostrated that they were compelled to disengage his feet from the stirrups. They carried him a few yards into the woods north of the turnpike to shield him from the expected advance of the Federalists. One was sent for an ambulance and a surgeon, while another stripped his mangled arm in order to bind up the wound. The warm blood was flowing in a stream down his wrist. His clothes impeded all access to its source, and nothing was at hand more efficient than a penknife to remove the obstruction.

Just at this moment Gen. Hill appeared upon the scene with a part of his staff. They called upon him for assistance. One of his staff, Maj. Leigh, succeeded in reaching the wound and staunching the blood with a handkerchief. It was at this moment that two Federal skirmishers approached within a few feet of the spot where he lay, with their muskets cocked. They little knew what a prize was in their grasp. When, at the command of Gen. Hill, two orderlies arose from the kneeling group and demanded their surrender, they seemed amazed at their nearness to their enemy, and yielded their arms without resistance.

Lieut. Morrison, suspecting from their approach that the Federalists must be near at hand, stepped out into the road to examine, and by the light of the moon he saw a cannon pointing toward them, apparently not more than 100 yards distant. Indeed, it was so near that the orders given by the officers to the cannoneers could be distinctly heard. Returning hurriedly, he announced that the enemy were planting artillery in the road and that the general must be immediately removed.

Gen. Hill now remounted and hurried back to make arrangements to meet this attack. In the combat which ensued, he himself was wounded a few moments after, and compelled to leave the field. No ambulance or litter was yet at hand, and the necessity for immediate removal suggested that they should bear the general away in their arms. To this he replied that if they would assist him to rise, he would walk to the rear. He was accordingly raised to his feet, and leaning upon the shoulders of two of his staff, he went slowly out of the highway, and toward his own troops.

The party was now met by a litter, which someone had sent from the rear, and the general was placed upon it and borne along by two of his officers. Just then the enemy fired a volley of canister shot up the road, which passed over their heads, but they proceeded only a few steps before the charge was repeated with more accurate aim. One of the officers bearing the litter was struck down, when Maj. Leigh, who was walking by their side, prevented the general from being precipitated to the ground. Just then the roadway was swept by a hurricane of projectiles of

The Last Meeting of Lee and Jackson
at Chancellorsville.

every species, before which it seemed no living thing could survive.

The bearers of the litter and all the attendants except Maj. Leigh and the general's two aids left him and fled into the woods on either side to escape the fearful tempest, while the sufferer lay along the road with his feet toward the foe, exposed to all its fury. It was now that his three faithful attendants displayed a heroic fidelity which deserves to go down with the immortal name of Jackson into future ages.

Disdaining to save their lives by deserting their chief, they lay down beside him in the causeway and sought to protect him as far as possible with their bodies. On one side was Maj. Leigh, and on the other Lieut. Smith. Again and again was the earth around them torn with volleys of canister, while shells and minie balls flew hissing over them, and the stroke of the iron hail raised sparkling flashes from the flinty gravel of the roadway. Gen. Jackson struggled violently to rise, as though to endeavour to leave the road, but Smith threw his arm over him and with friendly force held him to the earth, saying, "Sir, you must lie still; it will cost you your life if you rise." He speedily acquiesced, and lay quiet, but none of the four hoped to escape alive. Yet, almost by miracle, they were unharmed, and after a few moments the Federalists, having cleared the road of all except this little party, ceased to fire along it, and directed their aim to another quarter.

They now arose and resumed their retreat, the general walking and leaning upon two of his friends, proceeded along the gutter at the margin of the highway in order to avoid the troops, who were again hurrying to the front. Perceiving that he was recognized by some of them, they diverged still farther into the edge of the thicket. It was here that Gen. Pender of North Carolina, who had succeeded to the command of Hill's division upon the wounding of that officer, recognized Gen. Jackson, and said, "My men are thrown into such confusion by this fire that I fear I shall not be able to hold my ground."

Almost fainting with anguish and loss of blood, he still replied, in a voice feeble but full of his old determination and authority, "Gen. Pender, you must keep your men together and hold your ground." This was the last military order ever given by Jackson.

Gen. Jackson now complained of faintness, and was again placed upon the litter, and after some difficulty, men were obtained to bear him. To avoid the enemy's fire, which was again sweeping the road, they made their way through the tangled brushwood, almost tearing his clothing from him, and lacerating his face in their hurried progress. The foot of one of the men bearing his head was here tangled in a vine, and he fell prostrate. The general was thus thrown heavily to the ground upon his wounded side, inflicting painful bruises on his body and intolerable agony on his mangled arm, and renewing the flow of blood from it.

As they lifted him up he uttered one piteous groan, the only complaint which escaped his lips during the whole scene. Lieut. Smith raised his head upon his bosom, almost fearing to see him expiring in his arms, and asked, 'General, are you much hurt?' He replied, 'No, Mr. Smith, don't trouble yourself about me.' He was then replaced a second time upon the litter, and under a continuous shower of shells and cannon balls, borne a half mile farther to the rear, when an ambulance was found, containing his chief of artillery, Col. Crutchfield, who was also wounded. In this he was placed and hurried toward the field hospital, near Wilderness Run. From there he was taken to a farmhouse, his left arm amputated, and a few days afterward he died. His wife and little child were with him.

Thus ended the life of one of the world's greatest warriors and one of Christ's greatest soldiers.

The following ode to Stonewall Jackson was written by a Union officer (Miles O'Reiley), and is inserted here in preference to others that may have been quite as appropriate, because of the added beauty of sentiment it conveys from the fact that its author wore the blue:

He sleeps all quietly and cold
Beneath the soil that gave him birth;
Then break his battle brand in twain,
And lay it with him in the earth.

No more at midnight shall he urge
His toilsome march among the pines,
Nor hear upon the morning air
The war shout of his charging lines.

No more for him shall cannon park
Or tents gleam white upon the plain;
And where his camp fires blazed of yore,
Brown reapers laugh amid the grain!

No more above his narrow bed
Shall sound the tread of marching feet,
The rifle volley and the crash
Of sabres when the foeman meet.

Young April o'er his lowly mound
Shall shake the violets from her hair,
And glorious June with fervid kiss
Shall bid the roses blossom there.

And white-winged peace o'er all the land
Broods like a dove upon her nest,
While iron War, with slaughter gorged,
At length hath laid him down to rest.

And where we won our onward way,
With fire and steel through yonder wood,
The blackbird whistles and the quail
Gives answer to her timid brood.

And oft when white-haired grandsires tell
Of bloody struggles past and gone,
The children at their knees will hear

I have only referred incidentally to Jackson's Valley Campaign. It was short, but intensely dramatic. For bold maneuvering, rapid marching and brilliant strategy, I believe it has no parallel in history. As for results, without it Richmond doubtless would have been in the hands of McClellan in the spring of 1862.

Perhaps it is not extravagant to say that as the tidings reached the people all over the South that their idol was dead, more sorrow was expressed in tears than was ever known in the history of the world at the loss of any one man.

As the Israelites saw Elijah depart they exclaimed, "*The chariots of Israel and the horsemen thereof!*"

The South felt that in the loss of Stonewall Jackson they were parting with the "better half" of their army.

The North had the men, the money and the munition of war, but the South had Lee and Stonewall Jackson. And in having them they felt that they were more than a match for the North. Now that Jackson was gone the question was, What will Gen. Lee do?

To go back to the valley, I was indebted to my friend Faunt Neal for the loan of a horse, he being fortunate enough to have two.

After the Battle of Chancellorsville almost the entire force in the valley passed over the Blue Ridge and joined Lee's army on the Rappahannock. Of course, this included my command.

Lee's army still occupied the south bank of the Rappahannock, near the late battlefield, while just opposite, on the north bank, was the Union army waiting to see what the next move would be. I believe I have mentioned the fact that Gen. J.E.B. Stuart commanded Lee's entire cavalry force, about 10,000 men with several batteries of artillery. This force was encamped higher up the river, in Culpeper County, in and around Brandy Station, and might be called the left wing of Lee's army, although separated from it by several miles. Just opposite Stuart's cavalry and on the north bank of the river was the entire cavalry force of the Union army, supported by a corps of infantry.

CHAPTER 6

From Chancellorsville to Gettysburg

It was the wild midnight—
The storm was on the sky;
The lightning gave its light,
And the thunder echoed by.

After resting awhile and mourning the loss of our great soldier, Lee's army began to move. The question was (not only on our side of the river, but on the other), "What is Gen. Lee up to now?"

The Northern commander determined to investigate, and early in the morning of the ninth of June, 1863, a portion of the Union army began to cross the Rappahannock at every ford for miles, up and down the river.

I was on picket at one of the fords, and was relieved at 3 o'clock in the morning, another soldier taking my place.

I went up through the field into the woods where our reserves (some 20 men) were in camp. It was from this squadron that pickets were sent out and posted along the river.

I hitched my horse, and wrapped in a blanket, lay down to sleep. But I was soon rudely awakened by the watchman, who shouted that the enemy was crossing the river. We all jumped up and mounted our horses. Our captain was with us.

The day was just breaking. The pickets were hurrying up from the river in every direction, firing their pistols to give the alarm.

Our captain formed the men in the edge of the woods for

the purpose of checking for a few minutes the advancing enemy, so as to give the 10,000 cavalrymen that were encamped a mile or so in the rear time to saddle and mount their horses and prepare for battle.

The enemy came pouring up from the river, and we opened fire on them, checking them for the moment. Two of our men were killed, several wounded, and two horses killed.

Two couriers had gone ahead to arouse the camp. We soon followed them along the road through the woods, the enemy hard on our heels.

I was riding with the captain in the rear. We were not aware that the Yankees were so close to us, and the captain was calling to the men to check their speed. I looked behind, called to the captain and told him they were right on us, and just as I spoke two bullets went hissing by my head. The captain yelled to his men to move forward, and bending low on the necks of our horses, we gave them the spur.

As we came out of the woods into the fields we met the Sixth Virginia (my regiment), under Col. Flournoy, coming down the road at full gallop. Just on his left, and almost on a line with the Sixth, was the Seventh Regiment coming across the fields (for there were no fences then). These two regiments entered the woods, one on the right and one on the left, and stretching out on either side, poured a volley into the advancing enemy that caused them to halt for awhile.

The roar of the guns in the woods at that early hour in the morning was terrific. What was going on in front of us was being enacted up and down the river for at least three miles.

Our forces then fell back into the open country, and the battle continued, at intervals, all day long.

The Yankees were supported by infantry, while we had nothing but cavalry and artillery.

Our enemies could have driven us back farther if they had tried to, but they seemed to be afraid of getting into trouble. I do not know what our commander, Gen. Stuart, knew, but I did not suppose that Gen. Lee was within 30 miles of us. Toward sunset I saw him come riding across the fields on his gray horse, "Traveller," accompanied by his staff. He seemed as calm and unconcerned as if he were inspecting the land with the view of a purchase.

Whether it was the presence of Gen. Lee himself, or the fear that he had his army with him, I know not, but simultaneously with the appearance of Gen. Lee the enemy began to move back and recross the river. We did not press them, but gave them their own time.

We re-established our picket line along the river, and everything was quiet for a day or two.

We went down the next day to the spot where the first fight took place, and found our two men lying dead by the side of a tree, and several dead horses. The enemy had removed their dead (if they had any). It was too dark when we were fighting for us to see whether we did any execution or not at this particular point. We buried our two men where they fell and went back to camp. Total losses as reported by each side—Confederate, 485; Federal, 907.

The next day we were quietly resting in the woods, watching the infantry as they tramped by all day long, moving in a northeasterly direction. The question was asked 10,000 times perhaps that day, "What is Marse Robert up to now? Where is he taking us?" (Gen. Lee was called Marse Robert by his soldiers.)

In the afternoon we noticed a long string of wagons of a peculiar construction, each drawn by six horses, and loaded with something covered with white canvas. Of course, we were all curious to know what these wagons contained. The secret soon leaked out. They were pontoon bridges. And then we began to speculate as to what rivers we were to cross. Some said we were destined for the Ohio, others for the Potomac.

Just before sunset the bugle sounded "saddle up," and soon Stuart's cavalry was in the saddle and on the march.

Everything was trending one way, namely, northeast.

The infantry went into camp at night, but the cavalry marched through most of the night, crossing the Rappahannock several miles above where we had been fighting.

Lee's entire army was *en route* for Pennsylvania, as we afterward learned, the cavalry keeping in between the two armies, protecting the wagon trains and concealing, as far as possible, our army's destination.[1]

The infantry, artillery and baggage train crossed the Blue Ridge at the various gaps, fording the Shenandoah River, and moved down the valley of Virginia toward the Potomac.

Lee's cavalry kept on the east side of the mountain, holding the enemy back as much as possible.

When we reached Fauquier and Loudoun counties the Union cavalry made a desperate effort to drive in our cavalry and discover the route of our main army.

Heavy fighting began at Aldie, below Middleburg, and was continued up the pike through the town of Middleburg up as far as Upperville, where I had been captured the year before.

The enemy's cavalry was supported by infantry, and our forces fell back fighting foot by foot until they reached Upperville, where we met a division of infantry that Gen. Lee had sent to help us beat back the enemy. The Confederates who were killed in this action are buried in Middleburg and Upperville, in the cemeteries just outside of the two towns, and the ladies of these villages and the country round about were kept busy caring for the wounded.

---

1. The two armies, occupying opposite banks of the river near Fredericksburg, began their march for Gettysburg June the 3rd, 1863, moving northeast along the Rappahannock River, the cavalry of each army marching between. When Lee reached the Blue Ridge he crossed it at three different places, Chester Gap, Ashby's and Snickersville Gaps. The two cavalry forces came together and fought quite a severe battle, beginning at Aldie, below Middleburg, and extending to Paris, at the foot of the mountain. Directly after this battle Stuart took the main part of his cavalry, moved back as far as Salem, or Delaplane, as it is now called, moved across the country in rear of the Federal army, passing Manassas and Centerville, then marched direct for the Potomac, which he crossed between Leesburg and Washington. Then through Maryland into Pennsylvania as far as Carlisle, and there he turned south, arriving at Gettysburg on the night after the second day of the battle, thus completely encircling the Union army. (See map).

On its march down the Virginia valley to the Potomac Lee's army took 4000 prisoners, 25 cannon, 250 wagons, 400 horses, 269 small arms and quantities of stores.

I escaped some of the heaviest of this fighting by being detailed to guard the prisoners back to Winchester.

The night before the battle I was sent out along the road at the foot of the mountain to discover whether the enemy was approaching from that direction or not. After a lonely ride of several hours I came back and had a time finding Gen. Stuart, to whom I was instructed to report. I found him asleep on the porch of the home of Caleb Rector. I aroused him and delivered my message.

His reply was, "All right." I looked up my own command, and lay down for the remainder of the night.

Lee's army crossed the river at Williamsport, Md., on the pontoon bridge.[2] The Northern army crossed between Harper's Ferry and Washington, and our cavalry, strange to say, went below the Union army and crossed the river near Washington, thus circling the Union army and arriving at Gettysburg the last day of the battle. Stuart captured and destroyed many wagons and much property on this expedition.

My brigade of cavalry did not follow Stuart, but followed the main army, bringing up the rear.

After crossing the river, Lee led his main army straight for Chambersburg, Pa. I cannot describe the feeling of the Southern soldiers as they crossed the line separating Maryland and Pennsylvania, and trod for the first time the sacred soil of the North. Many of our soldiers had been on Maryland soil before this, and although Maryland was not a part of the Confederacy, we felt that she was one of us, and while marching over her roads and fields we were still in our own domain, but not so when we crossed into Pennsylvania.

We were then in the enemy's territory, and it gave us inexpressible joy to think that we were strong enough and bold

---

2. The map only shows one point where Lee crossed into Maryland, but the army divided before reaching the Potomac, one part crossing at Williamsport, and the other at Shepherdstown, and, uniting at Hagerstown, moved on toward Chambersburg. From this point, Lee sent a portion of Ewell's division as far north as Carlisle, while another portion marched to York, then to Wrightsville, on the Susquehanna River, all returning in time to meet the Union army at Gettysburg.

enough to go so far from home and attack our enemy upon his own soil. The joy of our soldiers knew no bounds. We were as light-hearted and as gay as children on a picnic, and we had no fear as to result of the move.

Marching along the pike one day, the cavalry halted, and just on our left there was a modest home of a farmer. The garden was fenced, and came out and bordered on the road. His raspberries were ripe, and our soldiers sat on their horses, and leaning over were picking the berries from the vines. One soldier was bold enough to dismount and get over into the garden. We saw the family watching us from the window. The impudence on the part of this soldier was a little too much for the farmer. He came out with an old-fashioned shotgun and berated us in a manner most vehement, but did not shoot.

This stirred the risibles of our soldiers to such an extent that the whole command broke out with loud laughter and hurrah for the brave farmer, who single-handed, and with a single-barrel shotgun, was defying the whole rebel horde. If the entire command had levelled its guns at him I think he would have stood his ground, but he could not stand our ridicule, so he went back into his house, and all was quiet again. Presently the command moved off, leaving what berries they did not have time to pick. From Chambersburg, Lee turned his columns southward and moved toward Gettysburg to meet the Union army that was advancing in the opposite direction. The armies met, and the whole world knows the result.

The battle lasted three days. The first two days were decidedly in favour of the Confederates. My command took an active part in the battle, and the adjutant of my regiment was killed, also several in my company, and some were badly wounded and had to be left. I was struck with a ball on the shoulder, marking my coat, and had a bullet hole through the rim of my hat; but as the latter was caused by my own careless handling of my pistol, I can't count it as a trophy.

As the years go by the students of history are more and more amazed at the boldness of Gen. Lee in placing his army of 75,000, some say 65,000, at Gettysburg,[3] when he knew that between him and the capital of the Confederacy (which his army was intended to protect) was the capital of the United States protected by an army of not less than 200,000 soldiers, and I might add by the best-equipped army in the world, for the United States Government had the markets of the world to draw supplies from.

In the morning of the third day of the battle of Gettysburg there had been a terrible artillery duel that made the earth tremble for miles around, and was heard far and wide.

When the guns got too hot for safety the firing ceased, the noise died away and the soldiers lay down to rest.

During this interval Gen. Lee called his generals together for counsel. They discussed the situation for some time, which had grown serious. Lee's losses had been heavy in killed and wounded, and his stock of ammunition was growing low.

After considerable discussion Lee mounted his gray horse, rode off a few paces to a slight elevation, and lifting his field glass to his eyes looked intently at the long lines of blue that stretched along the slopes, in the hope of finding some weak point which he might attack. Then returning to his officers he said in a firm voice: "We will attack the enemy's centre, cut through, roll back their wings on either side and crush or rout their army." Then he said: "Gen. Pickett will lead the attack."

Pickett was a handsome young Virginian, a splendid rider, a brave commander, and one of the most picturesque figures in the Confederate army. Bowing his head in submission, he mounted his horse, and tossing back his long auburn locks, rode off and disappeared among the trees. The other officers soon joined their several commands, and Gen. Lee was left alone with his staff.

There was ominous silence everywhere; even the winds had gone away, and the banners hung limp on their staffs. The birds

---

3. General Longstreet, in his book *From Manassas to Appomattox*, says the Confederate forces that crossed the Potomac were 75,568, and fixes the total of the Union army at 100,000, in round figures. General Meade's monthly returns for June 30, shows 99,131 present for duty and equipped at Gettysburg.

had all left the trees, the cattle had left the fields, and the small squadrons of cavalry that had been scouting between the two armies retired and took position on either flank. Yonder in front, stretching along the slopes, lay the blue lines of the enemy, like a huge monster asleep, while behind were the hilltops, all frowning with wide-mouthed cannon loaded to the lips.

Soon long lines of gray came stealing out of the woods like waves out of the sea. Long lines of gray moved over the fields like waves over the sea. These were Pickett's men; and Pickett, handsome Pickett, was at their head riding in silence.

The polished steel of the guns, as the lines rose and fell over the uneven ground, caught the rays of the bright July sun, developing a picture of dazzling splendour.

I wonder what was passing through the minds of those boys (their average age perhaps not much over twenty) as they moved step by step toward those bristling lines of steel in their front?

They were thinking of home. Far over the hills, "Way down south in Dixie."

Step by step came the gray, nearer and nearer, when suddenly there was a sound that shook the hills and made every heart quake. It was the signal gun.

Simultaneously with the sound came a cannon ball hissing through the air, and passing over the heads of the advancing columns, struck the ground beyond.

Then suddenly the whole slope was wreathed in smoke and flame, accompanied with a noise like the roar of a thousand cataracts.

Was it a huge volcanic eruption? No. The Blue and the Gray had met. The smoke rose higher and higher, and spread wider and wider, hiding the sun, and then gently dropping back, hid from human eyes the dreadful tragedy.

But the battle went on and on, and the roar of the guns continued. After a while, when the sun was sinking to rest, there was a hush. The noise died away. The winds came creeping back from the west, and gently lifting the coverlet of smoke, revealed a strange sight.

The fields were all carpeted, a beautiful carpet, a costly carpet, more costly than axminster or velvet. The figures were horses and men all matted and woven together with skeins of scarlet thread.

The battle is over and Gettysburg has passed into history.

The moon and the stars come out, and the surgeons with their attendants appear with their knives and saws, and when morning came there were stacks of legs and arms standing in the fields like shocks of corn.

The two armies confronted each other all day long, but not a shot was fired. Up to noon that day, I think I can safely say there was not a man in either army, from the commanders-in-chief to the humblest private in the ranks, that knew how the battle had gone save one, and that one was Gen. Robert E. Lee.

About 4 o'clock in the afternoon, while the cavalrymen were grazing their horses in the rear of the infantry, a low, rumbling sound was heard resembling distant thunder, except that it was continuous. A private (one of my company) standing near me stood up and pointing toward the battlefield said, "Look at that, will you?" A number of us rose to our feet and saw a long line of wagons with their white covers moving toward us along the road leading to Chambersburg.

Then he used this strange expression: "*That looks like a mice.*" A slang phrase often used at that time. He meant nothing more nor less than this: "We are beaten and our army is retreating."

The wagons going back over the same road that had brought us to Gettysburg told the story, and soon the whole army knew the fact. This is the first time Lee's army had ever met defeat.

It is said that the loss of the two armies was about 50,000. This probably included the prisoners; but there were not many prisoners taken on either side. The major portion of the losses were in killed and wounded.

The badly wounded were left on the field to be cared for by the enemy. Those who could walk, and those who were able to ride and could find places in the wagons, followed the retreating army.

The wagon train was miles and miles long. It did not follow the road to Chambersburg very far, but turned off and took a shorter cut through a mountainous district toward the point where the army had crossed the river into Maryland. This wagon train was guarded by a large body of cavalry, including my command.

Just as the sun was going down, dark ominous clouds came trooping up from the west with thunder and lightning, and it was not long before the whole heavens were covered and rain was falling in torrents.

I am not familiar with the topography of the country through which we retreated, but all night long we seemed to be in a narrow road, with steep hills or mountains on either side. We had with us a good many cattle with which to feed the army. These got loose in the mountains and hills covered with timber, and between their constant bellowing and the flashes of lightning and crashing thunder the night was hideous in the extreme. Wagons were breaking down, others getting stalled, and, to make matters worse, about midnight we were attacked by the Union cavalry.

This mountainous road came out on a wide turnpike, and just at this point Kilpatrick (commanding the Union cavalry) had cut our wagon train in two and planted a battery of artillery with the guns pointing toward the point from which we were advancing.

The cavalry which was stretched along the wagon train was ordered to the front. It was with great difficulty that we could get past the wagons in the darkness, and hence our progress was slow, but we finally worked our way up to the front and were dismounted and formed in line as best we could on either side of the road among the rocks and trees and then moved forward in an effort to drive the battery away from its position so we could resume our march. The only light we had to guide us was from the lightning in the heavens and the vivid flashes that came from the enemy's cannon. Their firing did not do much execution, as they failed to get a proper range. Besides, we were so close to them they were firing over our heads, but the booming of the guns that hour of night, with the roar of the thunder, was terrifying indeed, and beyond description. We would wait for a lightning flash and advance a few steps and halt, and then for a light from the batteries and again advance.

In the meantime day was breaking, and the light from the sun was coming in, and at this point our enemy disappeared and the march was resumed. We were afraid that the wagons that had already passed out on the open turnpike had been captured. There were about 200 of them, but such was not the case.

With these wagons was our brigadier commander, Gen. Wm. E. Jones, and two regiments of cavalry. They got so mixed up with the enemy's cavalry that night that it was almost impossible to distinguish friend from foe. Our general was a unique character, and many are the jokes that are told on him. While this fighting was going on those about him would address him as general. He rebuked them for this and said, "Call me Bill." The explanation was that the enemy was so close to them (in fact, mixed up with them) that they did not want him to know that there was a general in the crowd.

Two days afterwards we got hold of one of the county papers, which, in giving the account of this attack, stated that the rebel, Gen. Wm. E. Jones, was captured. Perhaps but for the shrewdness of Gen. Wm. E. Jones in having his men call him "Bill" instead of "General," it might have been true. The firing among the horses attached to the wagons that had gone out on the open pike frightened them to such an extent that they were stampeded, and we saw the next morning as we rode along that some of the wagons had tumbled over the precipice on the right, carrying with them the horses; also the wounded soldiers that were riding in the wagons.

The retreat was continued all the next day, the enemy's cavalry attacking us whenever they could, but without effect.

When we reached the river we found that our pontoon bridge had been partly swept away by the flood caused by the storm I have just spoken of. There was nothing to do but make a stand until the bridge could be repaired, or until the river should fall sufficiently to allow us to ford it.

My recollection is that we remained on that side of the river about a week. In the meantime the whole Northern army gathered in our front and threatened us with destruction, but they seemed to be about as afraid of us as we were of them; for instead of attacking us, they began to throw up breastworks in their front to protect themselves from attack. This greatly encouraged us, and even the privates in the ranks were heard to remark, "We're in no danger, they're afraid of us; look at their breastworks."

By the time the bridge was restored the river had fallen sufficiently to allow the cavalry to ford it. The army leisurely crossed, the infantry, artillery and wagons crossing on the bridge, while the cavalry waded through the water. The passage was made at night.

Gen. Meade, who commanded the Northern army, was very much censured for not attacking Lee while he was on the north side of the river. The Government at Washington seemed to think it would have resulted in the surrender of his army; but we in the ranks on the Confederate side had no fear of such a disaster.

It is true, we were short of ammunition, but the infantry had the bayonet and the cavalry the sabre, and we felt satisfied that we were not in much danger.

I neglected to say that as we marched through the towns of Pennsylvania it was distressing to see the sad faces of the populace as they gathered at their front doors and windows watching us as we moved through their streets. It resembled a funeral, at which all the people were mourners.

It was so different when we were marching through the cities and towns of the South. There we were greeted by the people with waving flags and smiling faces. Another thing we noticed which was quite different from what we witnessed in our own land was a great number of young men between the ages of 18 and 45 in citizen's clothes. This had a rather depressing effect upon us, because it showed us that the North had reserves to draw from, while our men, within the age limit, were all in the army.

It is said that misfortunes never come singly.

No sooner had we reached the south bank of the Potomac than we heard the distressing news that Vicksburg had fallen. This opened the Mississippi River to Farragut's fleet of warships stationed at the mouth of that river, and cut the Confederacy in two.

Then disaster followed disaster in that part of the field; but as I said in the beginning, I am not writing a history of the war, and hence will not attempt to follow the movements of the Western armies.

The question is often asked, "Why did Gen. Lee take his army into Pennsylvania?" That question is easily answered.

For the same reason that the children of Israel went down into Egypt. There was a famine in the land, and they went there for corn. Food was growing scarcer and scarcer in the South, and it became a serious question not only as to how the army was to be fed, but also the citizens at home, the old men, women and children.

No supplies could be brought from beyond the Mississippi. Tennessee and Kentucky were in the hands of the enemy, a great portion of Virginia; in fact, the richest farming sections were ravished first by one army, then by the other, making it impossible for the farmers to put in their grain or reap their harvests.

The other States of the South grew mostly cotton and tobacco. All the Southern ports were closely blockaded; hence the problem of sustaining human life was growing more serious every day.

If Gen. Lee had been successful at the battle of Gettysburg his army would have remained north of the Potomac until late in the fall, and would have subsisted upon the country surrounding his camps. At the same time, the farmers on the eastern side of the Blue Ridge and in the rich valley of Virginia could have planted and reaped an abundant harvest, which would have sufficed to have taken care of man and beast during the long winter months; but Providence ruled otherwise, and Lee was compelled to move his army back and provide for it as best he could.

Another question has been as often asked. "Why was Lee not successful at Gettysburg?" Gen. Lee seemed to have anticipated this question, and answered it in language almost divine when he said, "It was all my fault." He hoped this would have quieted criticism, but it did not, and for forty-odd years, (as at time of first publication), critics have been trying to fix the blame on someone.

Of course, I cannot solve the problem, but I would suggest this: Gen. Lee could not take the risk at Gettysburg that he took when he fought his other battles. He was too far from his base of supplies. If he had been defeated at Seven Pines, Manassas, Antietam, Fredericksburg, Chancellorsville, the Wilderness, Spotsylvania, Cold Harbor, he would have had the defences of Richmond to fall back upon. But not so at Gettysburg. If he should be defeated there he must retain an army strong enough to cut through the lines of the enemy, in order to reach his base of supplies.

After three days' fighting at Gettysburg he had gone as far as he dared go toward the depletion of his men and supplies; hence he ordered a retreat, knowing that he was still strong enough to handle the enemy and reach the south bank of the Potomac.

Some say it was because Jackson was not there; but the battles of the Wilderness, Spotsylvania and Cold Harbor, where Grant was in command of the Northern army, demonstrated that Lee could win victories without Jackson. Perhaps what contributed most to Lee's defeat at Gettysburg was the absence of the cavalry just at a time when he needed it most. Had Stuart kept the cavalry between the two armies, and informed Lee as to the movements of the enemy, he would not have been placed in such a disadvantageous position as he was at Gettysburg. Then again, the enemy had vastly superior numbers.

Whatever may have been the cause of his defeat, Gen. Lee, with the magnanimity characteristic of him, said: "It was all my fault."

GEN. ROBERT E. LEE.
This picture was taken at the rear of
General Lee's house on Franklin street,
Richmond, in April, 1865, immediately
after his return from Appomattox, and
represents him in the style of uniform
which he habitually wore in the army.

CHAPTER 7

From Gettysburg to the Wilderness

But who shall break the guards that wait
Before the awful face of Fate?
The tattered standards of the South
Were shrivelled at the cannon's mouth,
And all her hopes were desolate.

The main army marched slowly back up the valley, crossing at the various gaps east of Winchester, and occupied a position on the south bank of the Rapidan, a branch of the Rappahannock.

The cavalry under Stuart took the east side of the Blue Ridge and marched in a parallel line with the infantry. This took me by my old home. I could stop only for a few minutes. I remember that I was upbraided for my appearance and was compared to the *Prodigal Son*. But when I told them what I had passed through, they were ready to kill the fatted calf. I had, though, no time for this, as my regiment was on the march. Besides, I knew there was no calf.

The enemy kept at a safe distance, and did not molest us. We halted at Brandy Station, where we had fought the battle of June 9th, a month before. They halted at the Rappahannock and occupied both sides of the river.

The land for miles and miles around Brandy Station was almost level and entirely denuded of fences, the soldiers having used them for firewood. It was an ideal battlefield.

Here was the home of John Minor Botts, a distinguished

Virginian, respected and protected by the Northern army for his Union sentiments, and by the South for his integrity. He had a beautiful home and a fine, large estate, a choice herd of milch cows, and I have often gone there at milking time and got my canteen filled with milk just from the cow.

The price we paid was 25 cents a quart, in Confederate money. We thought it very cheap for such good, rich milk, and all of us had a good word to say for Mr. Botts and his family, even if they were Unionists.

Gen. Stuart threw out his pickets across the fields, and just in front of us the enemy did likewise. The pickets were in full view of each other, and a long-range musket might have sent a bullet across the line at any time, but we did not molest each other. At night the lines came still closer together, and we could distinctly hear them relieving their pickets every two hours, and they doubtless could hear us doing the same.

This state of things remained for several weeks. Not a shot was fired during all that time, and so well acquainted did the pickets of each army become, that it was not an uncommon thing to see them marching across the fields to meet each other and exchange greetings, and often the Confederates traded tobacco for coffee and sugar. I took quite an interest in this bartering and trading. This got to be so common that Gen. Stuart had to issue an order forbidding it.

After a while conditions changed. Gen. Lee had sent Longstreet's corps to Tennessee to reinforce Bragg, weakening his army to the extent of 20,000 men. Probably for this reason the enemy determined to make a demonstration, and began a movement toward our front. But so considerate were they that they did not open fire on us until we had gotten beyond range of their guns. This fraternal condition perhaps never existed before between two contending armies.

As they advanced we gradually fell back, and when we had retreated about a mile, they began firing on us. The friendly sentiment was soon dissipated, we returned the fire, and began to dispute their passage. But as they had a much larger force we gradually released the territory, fighting as we retreated.

My part of the line carried me directly through the streets of Culpeper, and the fighting in and around the town was the heaviest that we encountered. Several of our men had their horses killed, and I saw the enemy's cavalry pick the men up as they ran in their effort to escape.

We continued to fall back until we reached the Rapidan. Here Gen. Lee was strongly entrenched, and the enemy, after remaining in our front for some days, fell back to their old position on the Rappahannock. There was one item of interest which I neglected to mention in its proper place, and that was an address which Gen. Lee issued to his soldiers after his long march back from Gettysburg. It was printed on paper, about the size of a half sheet of note paper. It began with these words:

To the Soldiers of the Army of Northern Virginia:
Soldiers, we have sinned.

I cannot remember any more of the address, but those words have lingered lovingly in my memory ever since. Each soldier was handed one of these papers, and I am ashamed to say I did not keep my copy, and do not know of anyone who did.

Shortly after this demonstration of the Union army, Gen. Lee made an advance, but not directly in front. He moved his army toward the northeast, and his efforts seemed to have been to make a flank movement and get in the enemy's rear, just as had been done the year before when Jackson got in the rear of Pope at Manassas. The cavalry remained to watch the enemy's front, and prevent a move toward Richmond.

After Lee had gotten well on his march the cavalry crossed the river and began to drive in the enemy's outposts and press them back toward Culpeper, and then on through Culpeper to Brandy Station, where the enemy made a stand.

A short distance beyond the station was a slight elevation running across our front, completely hiding the movements of the enemy. As there was no elevation anywhere that we might occupy and see beyond the ridge in our front, all we could see was the large force occupying the crest of the ridge. We were afraid to charge, for fear of running into their whole army.

After a good deal of manoeuvring and waiting we saw the long lines of Union cavalry coming over the ridge and moving toward us in the line of battle. Closer and closer they came, and when they got within 200 yards of us, their leader ordered a charge, and it looked as if the whole column was coming right into our ranks.

I have a vivid recollection of the scene. I noticed as they approached that quite a number of them, perhaps every third man, was reining in his horse, which meant, "I have gone as far as I mean to go." Of course, what I saw my comrades saw, and we knew at once, by this action, they were whipped; but the others came on, dashing right into our ranks, firing as they came. The dust and smoke from the guns made it almost impossible to distinguish friend from foe, but I noticed close to me a large Union officer, riding a splendid horse, with his sabre over his head, calling his men to follow him. I had my sabre drawn, and I raised it over his head, but did not have the heart to hit him. Somehow or other, my arm would not obey me. It seemed too much like murder.

But Lieut. Armistead (an officer in my company) was not so chicken-hearted, but spurred his horse, "Long Tom," up until his pistol almost touched the officer, and shot him in the side. I saw him fall from his horse, and afterward attempt to get up. Then I lost sight of him. It was said to be Gen. Baker of the Union army, who was in command of the forces making the attack. We took some prisoners, others in the confusion, amid the dust and smoke, fled and escaped within their own lines. Then there was a halt for an hour or more.

Several fresh regiments of our cavalry came up and took positions, ready for attack or defence, whichever it might be.

What troubled our command was to know what was beyond that ridge. We were afraid to move forward, for fear of running into ambush.

Presently we saw a magnificent sight. The colonel of the

Fourth Virginia Regiment, mounted on a beautiful black horse, moved forward, calling upon his regiment to follow him. It was Colonel, afterward General, Rosser.

As the regiment moved toward the enemy's lines, at a gallop, the cry went up and down the ranks, "Look at Rosser, look at Rosser." Everybody expected to see him tumble from his horse, shot to death. But he went forward, leading his men, and when the enemy discovered that we were coming in earnest, they turned on their heels and fled. Other regiments followed in rapid succession, and when we had gotten on top of the ridge we found that the enemy was disappearing in the distance as fast as their flying horses could carry them. We afterward learned that their stand at Brandy Station was only intended to check our forces until theirs could get across the Rappahannock River, about three miles distant.

After this fracas was over we began to look about us to see whether any of us showed marks of the strife. I found a bullet hole through the strap that held my sabre to my belt, and as the strap laid close to my side, it was allowed to pass as a "close shave." But the greatest danger I was in, I think, was from the sabre of Gen. Baker. A right cut from that strong arm of his could have severed my head.

There was one of our command who was shot in the neck, and an artery cut. The blood spurted out like water from a spigot. He dismounted and stood by his horse until, weakened by the loss of blood, he fell to the ground. He realized, as everyone else did, that he was beyond human aid. As Solomon put it in Ecclesiastes, "The golden bowl had been broken."

But to go back. Early in the day, when we were driving the enemy from our front, the cavalry dismounted and fought on foot. This was often done, as the men can do better execution when on the ground, and, besides, they are better protected from the fire of the enemy. On foot, you have to protect you the trees and the rocks and the fences, every little hillock; in fact, anything else that would stop a bullet, but on horseback you are a splendid target for the sharpshooter. Hence, the cavalry on some occasions preferred to be on foot. But when there was any retreating to do, like Richard III, they wanted a horse.

On this particular occasion I was among those chosen to lead the horses. In fact, it always fell to the fourth man. He sat on his horse, while the other three men dismounted and went to the front. These were called the led horses, and, of course, they followed in the rear, keeping as much out of danger as possible.

As we moved along through the fields we passed a small dwelling; I halted in front of the door and asked the good lady of the house for something to eat. She came out, trembling from head to foot, with two other ladies, who I presume were her daughters, and gave me some bread.

Seeing the long string of led horses, she asked in the most distressed tone if all the men belonging to those horses had been killed. I explained the meaning of the horses being led, and assured her they were in no danger, as the enemy was retreating rapidly in our front, and all danger had passed.

Just an hour before this the conditions were reversed. I was on foot, and on the firing line, and another was leading my horse.

We had taken shelter behind a low-railed fence, against which the Yankees, who had just left it, had thrown the earth as a protection. We were all lying down close to the ground and firing over the top of this obstruction, when a shell came hissing across the field, striking the breastwork a short distance from where I lay, scattering the rails and dirt in every direction. I remarked that as lightning never struck twice in the same place, that was the safest spot to get, and I began to crawl toward it. I had hardly moved a yard when another shell struck in this very same spot, verifying the old adage, that *there are exceptions to all rules.*

We were ordered to move forward from this position across the open field, which we did, the bullets buzzing past our ears like so many bees. We went a few hundred yards and then lay down flat on the ground in the grass, and continued firing at the puffs of smoke in our front, as that was all we could see. The enemy was lying as flat to the ground as we were. A great deal of this kind of fighting is done in this way. It doesn't rise to the dignity of a battle, but is called skirmishing.

One poor fellow lying next to me was struck by a bullet with a dull thud, that caused him to cry out in pain, and as we moved forward I saw him writhing in agony. I presume he was not mortally wounded, as mortal wounds do not cause much or any pain.

In the meantime, our enemy crept away from our front, and mounting their horses, galloped off. We followed in hot pursuit.

But to return to where we left our friends (the enemy crossing the Rappahannock). We did not pursue them beyond the river, but moved northeast, crossing the river at the same place where we had crossed on the march to Gettysburg. It was about 9 o'clock at night; beyond we could see all the hills brilliantly illuminated with camp-fires. It was a gorgeous spectacle.

As we had driven the enemy across the river a few miles below, of course, we in the ranks, concluded that these were the camp-fires of the enemy, and that a night attack was to be made upon their camp. But we crossed, notwithstanding, and as we rode up to the blazing fires we discovered that we were right in the midst of Lee's infantry.

We went into camp for the night. Early in the morning we were in the saddle, with both cavalry and infantry on the march. Marching parallel to us was the whole Union army. They were making for the defences of Washington, and we were trying to cut them off.

When we got as far as Bristoe Station, not far from Manassas, Gen. Lee made a swoop down upon them and tried to bring them to battle, but they were too swift for us. We did, however, have quite a severe fight at Bristoe Station between the advance guard of our army and the rear of the enemy.

Gen. A.P. Hill, commanding one of Lee's corps, made the attack. It was very severe while it lasted, and the roar of the musketry was terrific. But the enemy got away.

After it was over one of my company (Frank Peak) heard Gen.

Lee severely reprimand Gen. A.P. Hill in these words: "Gen. Hill, your line was too short and thin." I presume Gen. Lee thought if Gen. Hill had extended his line farther out, he might have captured the entire force in our front.

In this battle Rev. A.W. Green (to whom I have already referred as being captured at Harper's Ferry by Jackson) had one of his fingers shot off. I have often joked him and said it was I who shot it off. Just as I am writing this Mr. Green, whom I have not seen for 10 years, came into my office, and I told him what I was doing. He held up his hand, minus one finger, and said, "Yes, you did that."

We followed the retreating enemy some distance below Manassas, but could not overtake them. We halted for awhile, and a few days afterward the whole army, cavalry, infantry and artillery, marched slowly back toward the Rapidan.

The expedition was fruitless. The infantry, as is nearly always the case, marched with the wagon-trains, while the cavalry, in nearly every instance, leaves the wagons behind, depending upon whatever can be picked up from the farmers or the enemy.

In this particular section at this time, the farmers had no chance to plant crops. The trees had already been stripped of fruit. We could not even find a persimmon, and we suffered terribly with hunger. Of course, there was plenty of grass for the horses, but the men were entirely destitute of provisions.

We were looking forward to Manassas with vivid recollections of the rich haul that we had made there just prior to the second battle of Manassas, and everybody was saying, "We'll get plenty when we get to Manassas." We were there before we knew it. Everything was changed. There was not a building anywhere. The soil, enriched by the debris from former camps, had grown a rich crop of weeds that came half way up to the sides of our horses, and the only way we recognized the place was by our horses stumbling over the railroad tracks at the junction. It was a grievous disappointment to us.

While fighting just below Manassas, the enemy threw a shell in among the led horses, which burst and killed several of them.

A short time after that, while lying in camp, our stomachs crying bitterly for food, someone suggested we try horse flesh. I remember pulling out my knife and sharpening it on a stone preparatory to cutting a steak from one of the dead horses, but just at this point a caravan on horseback arrived with a supply of food. We had a rich feast, and were happy again.

I do not know where the Union army halted in their retreat toward Washington, but in a day or two after this, Lee moved his entire army back toward its old camp on the Rapidan, as I have just said.

I think this was early in November. We felt winter approaching, and I remember when we reached the Rappahannock, although there was a bridge a mile below, the cavalry forded the stream, the men getting wet above their knees, as the water came well up to the sides of the horses. Gen. Lee, noticing that the men were wet from fording the river, said to our brigade commander (Gen. Lomax) in a kind and fatherly tone, "My! General, you should have used the bridge below." I suppose Gen. Lomax thought that as we were soldiers we ought not to mind a little wetting, even if the cold November winds were blowing.

My recollection is that the whole army, infantry, cavalry and artillery, encamped in and around Brandy Station and prepared for winter. The infantry began to build little low huts, the cracks filled up with mud and tops covered with slabs split from logs.

Every mess had its own hut. The cavalry, knowing that they would likely be kept on the march, made no preparation for winter.

Sometime after this (I can't remember just how long) orders came to break camp and move back on the south side of the Rapidan. I do not know what commotion this move caused in the ranks of the infantry, but we cavalrymen, who remained for some time in that neighbourhood and saw the deserted villages, sympathized with the infantry in the loss of their homes. But as the Six Hundred remarked, "*It is not for us to ask the reason why, but to do and die.*"

Mrs. R.E. Lee,
Wife of Gen. R.E. Lee, taken from an
old photograph soon after the close of the
war. The spots are result of defects on the
original photograph.

Shortly afterward the cavalry withdrew to the south bank of the Rapidan, near the infantry. I think this was in Orange county, near Orange Courthouse, probably half a mile from the river.

Sometime in January a courier came in from the front across the river and reported that the enemy's cavalry had been seen a few miles below, moving toward our camp.

The bugles sounded "saddle up" all through the camp, and several regiments of cavalry were soon in line and crossing the river. They dismounted, formed in line of battle, and moved across the fields. We soon found the enemy in our front, also dismounted, and firing began. We were ordered to fall back gradually toward the river, fighting as we retreated, the object being to draw the enemy toward the batteries that were on the opposite side of the river.

As we neared the banks of the river where the led horses were, our purpose was to remount and to cross the river, but the enemy pressed us so close that some of us, I among them, were compelled to cross on foot. This was rather a chilly experience, when you consider that it was the middle of January. But we got over, and our batteries opened fire on the enemy and compelled them to fall back.

Just as we came out of the river we met the infantry coming down and taking position behind the breastworks that had been thrown up along the south bank of the river. Those who had forded the river were allowed to go to camp, a short distance off, to dry their clothes, for it was freezing weather.

I had mounted my horse, and as I passed the column of infantry coming down to the river, a bullet fired by the enemy's sharpshooter on the opposite side struck one of the men, and he fell in a heap, dead, at the feet of my horse. He dropped as suddenly as if he had been taken by some powerful force and thrown violently to the ground. Every joint and muscle in his body seemed to have given way in an instant.

After we had dried our clothes before the camp-fire our command re-crossed the river to find out what the enemy proposed to do. We were again dismounted and formed in line across the field as before, and, moving forward, found the enemy just beyond the reach of our batteries. Lying close to the ground we began firing at each other, continuing long after dark. Then the firing ceased. After remaining there for some time, someone in command (I don't know who it was) ordered Capt. Gibson of our company to send four men with instructions to creep up as near as they could to the enemy's lines, stay there, and report whenever the enemy withdrew.

I was selected as one of the four men. When we got pretty near their line we got down flat on the ground, and like so many snakes crawled along until we got as close as we dared. We could distinctly see them on their horses, but we did not remain long before we saw them withdraw. We heard their officers giving the command.

We then came back, and had some difficulty getting in without being shot, from the fact that the regiment to which we belonged had been withdrawn and another put in its place, and the men did not seem to understand that we were out on this mission. We made our report, and shortly afterward mounted, re-crossed the river and went into camp. It proved to be nothing more than a reconnoissance of the enemy's cavalry, probably to find out whether Lee's army was still encamped on the river.

Sometime after this, perhaps two or three weeks, while on picket some miles up the river, a considerable distance from the main army's encampment, a body of the enemy's cavalry crossed the river somewhere between the pickets, and got behind the line of pickets unobserved.

It was a very foggy morning. Our post consisted of six men, and our position was a few hundred yards back of the river.

Two of the men were on picket; the others were at the post.

About 6 o'clock in the morning we heard a few shots in our rear. One of our men was sent back to find out the cause of it. He had not been gone many minutes when we heard other shots, which forced us to the conclusion that the enemy in some way had gotten behind us. Our pickets had also heard the firing, and came in to find out what the trouble was.

We followed the direction of the shots, and had not gone far before we saw through the heavy fog quite a large body of cavalry.

Whether friend or foe, it was impossible to determine. So we thought discretion the better part of valour and immediately turned, each fellow taking care of himself.

Three went up the river. Faunt Neal and myself took the opposite course. The Yankees (for it proved to be the enemy) had seen us, and started in pursuit. Neal and I rushed down the hill toward the river, passing a grove of small pine trees. My comrade turned abruptly to the right and hid himself in this sanctuary, while I continued across the meadow and up the hill on the opposite side into the woods and escaped.

We all turned up in camp the next day except one. He had ridden straight into the enemy's lines, thinking they were Confederates. This ended his military career.

I think it was about the first of February an order had been sent from headquarters allowing a certain number of regiments a furlough. It extended to my regiment. Some of the companies could not avail themselves of it, because their homes were wholly in the territory occupied by the enemy. My company was among the fortunate ones, although many of our men were from Loudoun and Fauquier, and the enemy was occupying part of this territory and making frequent raids through the other portions. But our officers stood sponsor for us, and we started for our respective homes as happy as children let out of school.

Those of us living in Loudoun and Fauquier had to observe the greatest caution to keep from being picked up by the enemy's scouting cavalry before reaching home. But there were no misfortunes, and with joy unspeakable, we, one by one, reached the "Old Homesteads."

To attempt to express the pleasure we got out of this little vacation would tax the English language severely.

'Tis true that these were not just the old homes we had left three years before in our bright new uniforms, with well-groomed horses and full haversacks. The marching and counter-marching of first one army, then the other, destroying fences and barns and driving off cattle and horses, made a great change in the appearance of things.

No one attempted to keep up appearances. Besides, at this time, nearly every home mourned one or more dead. The most of my old schoolmates who had crossed the Potomac *en route* for Gettysburg went down on that hot July afternoon when Pickett made his famous charge, for the Eighth Virginia Infantry, in which nearly all my schoolmates had enlisted, was almost annihilated that bloody afternoon.

Among the killed was Edwin Bailey, whom I have already mentioned as going out with me from Middleburg in the spring of 1862, he to rejoin his regiment, and I to enlist in the Sixth Virginia Cavalry. By his side in that battle was his brother John. Edwin fell first, mortally wounded, and John, severely wounded, fell across him. Edwin said, "John, if you get home, tell them I died a Christian." These were his only and last words.

I have often used this incident as an exemplification of the claims of Christianity.

Notwithstanding all this, we enjoyed our vacation immensely, but there was not a day that we were not in danger of being surrounded and captured. The bluecoats were scouting through the country almost continuously in search of Mosby's "gang," as they called it. We had to keep on guard and watch the roads and hilltops every hour of the day. We had the advantage of knowing the country and the hiding places and the short cuts, and then we had our loyal servants, always willing to aid us to escape "them Yankees."

For instance, I made a visit to Sunny Bank, the home of my brother-in-law, E.C. Broun. My horse was hitched to the rack, and I was inside enjoying the hospitalities of an old Virginia home, when one of the little darkies rushed in and said, "Yankees." They were soon all around the house, but, before getting there, one of the servants took the saddle and bridle off my steed, hid them, and turned him loose in the garden, where he posed as the old family driving nag, while I went to the back porch, climbed a ladder, and lifting a trap-door, got in between the ceiling and the roof. The trap-door was so adjusted that it did not show an opening. The ladder was taken away, and there I stayed until the enemy departed. I got back home safely, eight miles off, and had other close calls, but owing to the fidelity of the coloured people, who were always on the watch, and whose loyalty to the Confederate soldiers, whether they belonged to the family in which they lived or not, was touching and beautiful beyond comprehension. They always called the Confederates "Our Soldiers," and the other side "Them Yankees."

About this time a new star appeared upon the field of Mars. John S. Mosby, a native of Warrenton, Fauquier county, Virginia, serving as lieutenant in the First Virginia Cavalry, was captured and put in prison in Washington in the old Capitol. He was not there long before he was exchanged, but while there his mind was busy. He conceived the idea that if he had a small body of men well armed and well mounted, and given an independent command, he could render the Confederacy great service by operating along the lines of the B. & O., the C. & O., and the Orange and Alexandria railroads, and also upon the enemy's supply trains, that were constantly moving to and fro up and down the valley and other sections. He reported his plan to Gen. Stuart when he got out of prison. Gen. Stuart favoured it, and referred it to Gen. Lee, and Gen. Lee referred it to the War Department at Richmond, resulting in Mosby's being commissioned a captain, with ten men detached from his regiment (the First Virginia Cavalry) with permission to increase the number by recruiting from the young men in the district where he operated.

Mosby lost no time in getting his little force together at some point in Loudoun County. His first expedition was to Fairfax Courthouse. His plan was to get as close to the enemy as he could, hide his men behind a hill or in a body of timber, and rush pell-mell upon a passing wagon-train, or a detachment of Union troops, stampede them and capture what he could. In this way he captured or destroyed a great many wagons, took horses, mules and prisoners by the thousands. My younger brother Richard joined this command in 1864, being a little over 17 years old.

It may seem strange to the present age that a country devastated as this portion of Virginia was at this time, with so many homes mourning the loss of their brave sons slain in battle, or maimed for life, with starvation almost staring them in the face, with the capital of their country besieged by great armies, with what we would call at this day deprivation and suffering incomparable, that the people could have any heart for festivities, such as dances and plays. But such was the fact. The soldiers during their furlough were received everywhere as heroes, and were banqueted and entertained as if peace and plenty reigned throughout the land. Many a parody like the following was gotten off: "There was a sound of revelry by night," and "*Les Miserables*" (Lee's miserables) had gathered there.

But it must be remembered that it was this spirit among the Southern people that made them endure their hardships and sustain the conflict as long as they did. It was the women standing loyally by their husbands, brothers and lovers that made the Southern soldiers ready to play or ready to fight, regardless of what they had in their haversacks or wore on their backs.

There was no fixed time for our furlough, but we had places of rendezvous where we were ordered to meet once a week to receive instructions. Finally the time came when we were summoned to collect at Upperville (near the home of our captain) for the march back to the army.

I do not remember the date, but it was early in March. I do remember the first encampment we made for the night. We got up the next morning with six inches of snow covering us, resulting in my horse getting a bad cold, for during our furlough he was housed in a warm stable. This cold never left him, and he died from the effects of it several months afterward.

We were ordered to report at Staunton, Va. It was a long march from Loudoun county, but we were used to long marches. When we arrived there we found our regiment awaiting us. Without even a day's rest we were ordered to Richmond, a still longer march, and after remaining there two weeks we were ordered to Fredericksburg. A line of this route drawn on the map would form almost a perfect letter C, and if it had not been for a small obstacle in our way, in all probability we would have continued the march, forming the letter O.

The obstacle in our way was Grant's army on the Rappahannock.

CHAPTER 8

From the Wilderness to James River

Turning his bridle, Robert Lee
Rode to the rear. Like waves of the sea,
Bursting the dikes in their overflow,
Madly his veterans dashed on the foe.

The army of Northern Virginia had met and defeated Mc-Dowell, McClellan, Pope, Burnside and Hooker, and caused the retirement of Meade, but the Government at Washington had at last found a soldier believed to be a full match for Gen. Lee.

Grant had been successful in the West, and his achievements had made him the Nation's idol, so he was brought to the East and placed in command of the army of the Potomac.

All during the late fall and winter and early spring he was preparing an immense army, whose rendezvous was on the Rappahannock and in the district about Culpeper Courthouse. It was a greater and better equipped army than that under Mc-Clellan in 1862. Then again, McClellan was an untried soldier, while Grant had won his spurs on more than one battlefield. So the North had a right to feel that Lee would be beaten and Richmond captured. Besides this great army, another 30,000 strong was marching up the James River, taking the same route McClellan took two years before.

Gen. Benj. F. Butler was its commander. The two armies were to unite and compel the surrender or evacuation of the Confederate Capital.

It was about the first of May when Grant began his movements toward Lee's front. At this time the whole cavalry force of Gen. Lee was encamped in a rich grazing district about five miles from Fredericksburg.

We had been there several weeks, our horses had been wading in grass up to their knees. They had shed their winter coats, and were looking fine, and seemed to be ready for the fray.

Our principal article of food was fresh fish, caught from the Rappahannock River.

As we loitered around the camp from day to day, speculating as to when we should be called to the front, and discussing what would be the result of the coming battle, we began to get restless, as soldiers will. They live on excitement, and the booming of guns and the rattling of musketry is the sweetest music they can hear.

One bright May morning (it must have been about the first day of the month) we saw a courier with his horse all flecked with foam as he came dashing into our camp. He halted and asked for Gen. Stuart's headquarters. It proved to be a messenger from Gen. Lee, and it meant that the death-struggle was about to begin.

Soon the bugles were sounding all through the camps the old familiar call, "Saddle up, saddle up." We mounted, and each company forming in line and counting off by fours, wheeled into columns of two and marched off toward what was afterward known as the Battlefield of the Wilderness.

We arrived at the position assigned us about dark, where we went into camp in the woods, tying our horses to the trees and building camp-fires to cook our supper. I had (like the boy in the parable of the loaves and fishes) in my haversack a few small fresh fish, and I was wondering whether they would be sweet or not. I remember distinctly laying them on the coals of fire to broil. It has been 43 years since then, (as at time of first publication), but I can assure you I can almost taste those fish today. I don't think I ever ate anything so sweet.

The next day we were in the saddle early. The cavalry formed the right wing of Lee's army. The battle lasted two days. The

GEN. FITZHUGH LEE,
Who commanded a division
of Gen. J.E.B. Stuart's cavalry.

cavalry fought almost entirely on foot. It was mostly in heavy timber and thick undergrowth.

The first day we did not see the enemy, but we knew he was there, for the woods were ringing with the sound of their guns, and bullets were hissing about our ears.

When we struck this heavy body of timber we found a narrow road running through it. We followed this road cautiously for two or three miles. My company was in front. About 200 yards in front of the company rode two soldiers, side by side. We knew somewhere in front of us was the enemy, and it was our mission to find him. Suddenly we heard two shots—*pop, pop*. We all knew what that meant. The armies of Lee and Grant had met, and as far as I know, these were the first two shots fired of the Battle of the Wilderness. They had come from the enemy's guns. They had seen our advance guard, and the shots meant, "so far shalt thou come, and no farther." We took the hint and halted.

The regiment was dismounted, and the led horses were taken back some distance; we deployed on the right and left of the road and awaited results; then moved forward until we discovered the enemy's line. We exchanged some shots, and began falling slowly back, while they advanced.

As we retired, their bullets were hissing through our ranks and cutting the bark from the trees and the twigs from the bushes, and now and then striking down our men.

My cousin, Dallas Leith, and myself stood together behind a tree for protection. As he fired, his head was exposed, and a bullet from the enemy's ranks just brushed his lips. He turned to me and said, "Wasn't that a close shave?" And at the same time a bullet grazed my finger as I fired.

We fell back through the timber to the edge of the open fields, and getting behind a rail fence, remained there until the enemy came up. We held our fire until they got close to us, when we poured a volley into their ranks that sent them scurrying back through the woods. We then climbed the fence and followed them up.

About 20 steps from the fence we saw two Yankees lying

mortally wounded. We gathered around them and asked them some questions about where they were from, and one of our men pulled a photograph from the pocket of one of them. It was a picture of a young girl, and one of the men said, "I guess that's his sweetheart." He opened his eyes and said with much difficulty, "No, it is my sister."

Our captain was standing by, and as the men were so close to our line, someone conceived the idea that they had come up to surrender, and one of them said to our captain, "Captain, these men came up to surrender, and were shot down." One of the Yankees denied the accusation with some feeling. They were both shot in the breast, and were bleeding profusely. It was very evident that they had but a short time to live.

The captain ordered them to be taken back to a place of safety. They begged to remain where they were, saying that they hadn't long to live, but they were taken back to a safer place.

We were again ordered forward, and kept on until we came in touch with the enemy, when the firing was resumed.

Dallas Leith and myself were again behind a tree. He was kneeling down loading his gun, when his head was again exposed, and a ball struck him in the forehead. It tore away a part of the bone, exposing his brain. I felt confident the boy was killed, and had no other thought than that of leaving him there, for we had all we could do to carry back the wounded, much less the dead.

We were then ordered to fall back, and someone more humane than I proposed that we carry his body back with us. I protested that it was impossible, but the others insisted, and, tying a handkerchief around his head, his hair drenched with blood, we picked him up and carried him back about a mile, when to our surprise we got into a road and there found an ambulance. Putting him in it, he was carried to the hospital, in the rear. Strange to say, he lived about ten days, giving his father time to come from Loudoun County to see him before he died. About this same time his younger brother Henry (at home) was blown to pieces by a shell that he had picked up in the field on his father's farm and was trying to open it, to see what was inside.

But to return to the battle. This state of things continued for two whole days, with little intermission. Sometimes, however, there was not a shot fired for an hour.

During one of these intervals I remember sitting down, leaning my back against a large tree, and began writing a letter to my folks at home. Capt. Gibson came up to me and said, "Young man, if you don't want to get shot, you'd better get on the other side of that tree, for somewhere just in front of us, and not a great distance off, is the enemy's skirmish line, and they may open fire at any moment." I moved behind the tree and resumed my writing, but was suddenly stopped by the sound of firing in our front, that caused us to creep farther back into the woods.

On another occasion we had fallen back out of the timber into the open fields, and were firing from behind a fence at the enemy in the woods, whom we could not see for the undergrowth. Our attention was called to a large body of cavalry on our left, apparently the enemy on mischief bent.

There are times in a battle when every private soldier on the firing line becomes a "Commander-in-Chief." It is when orders cannot be given, or would not be heard if they were. Each soldier seems to know intuitively what to do, and the whole line acts in concert.

At this particular time the body of cavalry on our left proved to be the bluecoats, moving toward our rear. It did not take long for the information to spread up and down the line, and at once every man in the ranks, in absence of any orders from headquarters, concluded that the thing to do was to fall back. So each soldier gave the order to himself, and quicker than it takes time to tell it, the line was moving back over the fields.

We had retreated perhaps 200 yards when the movement was noticed by Gen. Fitzhugh Lee. He came galloping toward us on his white horse, and with a voice that could be heard above the shots of the guns, he said, "What does this mean?" In reply, hundreds of hands pointed toward the enemy on our left, and some voices said, "They're getting in our rear." Gen. Lee said, "Tut, tut, tut; go back, go back." And without a word every man wheeled around and started back for the position he had left. Gen. Lee perhaps knew that there were forces enough there to take care of the enemy, who, as we saw it, was getting behind us.

As I said before, this kind of warfare continued for two days, and all the time it was going on we could hear the booming of the artillery on our left, telling us that Grant was doing all he could to beat back or break through Lee's lines, and we knew, too, that he was not accomplishing his purpose. We could always tell which way the battle was going by the direction from which the sound came.

The night of the second day Grant silently and rapidly withdrew the main portion of his army from Lee's front and marched toward Spotsylvania Courthouse, which was some distance to the right of where the cavalry was fighting.

His object was to surprise Gen. Lee, and get between him and Richmond. But Gen. Lee had anticipated that very movement, and when Grant's infantry moved forward at Spotsylvania Courthouse, he found Lee's army there confronting him. Then began the bloodiest battle of all the war, so it is said.

It was during the Battle of the Wilderness that Gen. Grant sent that famous dispatch to Washington, "I will fight it out on this line if it takes all summer." If he meant the line between his army and Lee's, he changed his mind within 24 hours. But if he meant a line stretching from Wilderness to Petersburg, he kept his word. It took him all summer to get his army south of the James River, and cost him the loss (it is said) of 100,000 soldiers.

He could have placed his army there without firing a shot by following the route taken by McClellan, but Grant well knew he must first cripple Lee's army before he could capture Richmond, and that he could afford to lose five men to Lee's one in doing it, and I presume he thought the district called the "Wilderness" a good place to begin the work.

While Grant's army was moving under the cover of night

and the dense forests toward Spotsylvania Courthouse, our cavalry also moved in the same direction. And when Grant ordered his lines forward the next morning, the first to receive them was our cavalry.

The enemy's cavalry still confronted us when we began fighting. It seemed to be the same old tactics that had been played for the last two days, except that it was a little fiercer.

Among the killed that day was a handsome young colonel of one of the regiments of our brigade. His name was Collins. I think he was a Georgian.

He was always dressed as if he were going to a reception. His complexion was as fair as a woman's. His hair was light. He habitually wore a clean white collar and a bright new uniform (something unusual among soldiers in the midst of an active campaign), but "death loves a shining mark," and he was taken off.

About 10 o'clock in the morning our cavalry was withdrawn from the front, and going back to our led horses we mounted and slowly rode back toward Spotsylvania Courthouse.

The country here was different from where we had been fighting the two days previous. Much of it was open fields, and the timbered part of it was not encumbered with undergrowth.

As we slowly fell back we looked behind us and saw a gorgeous sight. It was Grant's line of battle moving forward as if on "Dress Parade," their brass buttons and steel guns with fixed bayonets glistening in the sun, with their banners floating in the breeze. The first thought among the private soldiers was, "Has Grant stolen a march on Lee, and is Richmond doomed?" It certainly looked so at this moment, but we kept on falling back.

As we entered the woods we suddenly came upon Lee's infantry lying down in line of battle waiting the enemy's advance. As we approached them, word was passed up and down the line not to cheer the infantry. This was the custom in the face of a battle when the cavalry, retiring from the front, gave way to the infantry.

They opened their ranks and let us pass through, and we formed in line some distance behind them. The infantry was entirely concealed from the enemy's view, and up to this time I am quite sure that Grant did not know that he was facing Lee's army at Spotsylvania Courthouse. But he was soon to be undeceived in a manner most tragic.

Lee's infantry waited until the enemy was within 100 yards, and then, rising to their feet, poured a volley into their ranks that brought many of them to the ground, and sent the others back from whence they came. This was only the beginning of the battle.

Leaving the infantry to take care of that part of the field, the cavalry was moved a mile to the right and again dismounted, and moved forward until we came under fire of the enemy's guns. We laid down behind a rail fence and fired between the rails. A bullet struck a rail just in front of my head and knocked the dust and splinters in my face, almost blinding me for a little while. We did not remain there very long, but were soon ordered back, and as we moved across the open fields in full view of the enemy, they kept up an incessant fire, many of the shots taking effect.

We could see the Union officers on the little hills in every direction, with their field glasses to their eyes, trying to discover what was in front of them.

The cavalry retired from the field, leaving the infantry to do the rest. How well it was done the historian has tragically told the story. It was on this field that "Hancock, the superb," made eight distinct attacks on Lee's centre, and finally breaking his line of battle, rushed his troops by thousands into the breach, and for the moment it looked as if the Confederacy was doomed.

Gen. Lee, seeing the peril in which his army was placed, ordered forward Gordon's division (which he was holding in reserve), placed himself at the head of it, and was about to lead them into battle in order to restore his broken lines. Shells were falling about Gen. Lee and his life was in peril. One of the officers rode up to him and said, "Gen. Lee, this is no place for you;

you must go to the rear." His troops refused to go forward until Gen. Lee had retired from the front. One of the soldiers came forward, and taking the reins of Lee's horse, led him back. Then Gen. Gordon led his division forward, the enemy was driven back, the line was restored, and Gen. Lee's army was saved from destruction and another year added to the life of the Confederacy.

I heard Gen. Gordon in a lecture delivered at "Music Hall," Baltimore, some years ago, describing this event, say (as he stretched out his hands horizontally), "My dead were piled that high, and three days after the battle I saw wounded men trying to pull themselves from under the mass of the dead above them. And at one point the slopes were so slippery with blood that my soldiers could not stand until the ground had been carpeted with the bodies of their fallen comrades."

A tree about six inches in diameter standing in a field was literally cut down by bullets, not a shot from a cannon having been fired on that part of the field.

The *Standard Encyclopaedia* puts the strength of Grant's army at 150,000, but does not state how many men Lee had. Perhaps 75,000 would be a fair estimate. The same authority gives Grant's losses at the battle of the Wilderness as 18,000; Lee's at 11,000.[1]

The losses in the battle of Spotsylvania Courthouse, fought two days afterward, were as great, if not greater, than those of the Wilderness.

When the cavalry retired from the front they mounted their horses, and almost Lee's entire cavalry force, headed by their chief, Gen. J.E.B. Stuart, started in a bee line for Richmond, without halting a moment.

Gen. Sheridan, commanding Grant's cavalry, had passed

---

1. General Longstreet gives 63,998 as the total strength of Lee's army in this campaign. Longstreet was severely wounded at the Battle of the Wilderness by a bullet shot through the neck. Was carried from the field on a litter, and was unable to return to the army for several months. Lee had lost the services of Jos. E. Johnson, Jackson, Longstreet, and a few days later J.E.B. Stuart. These were his ablest lieutenants.

around our right wing with his whole command, and was heading toward the Confederate Capital.

I think it was about 4 o'clock in the afternoon when we started. Sheridan was several miles ahead of us. We marched all night. We overtook Sheridan at Hanover Junction, on the railroad leading to Richmond; not, however, until he had destroyed a large quantity of provisions stored there for Lee's army, a great loss to the Confederates at that time.

Sheridan had prepared for this expedition, and all of his men had well-filled haversacks, while ours were empty.

I cannot remember just when and where we got in front of Sheridan, but I know from Hanover Junction on we were in constant touch with his forces, and harassed them all we could.

At a place called "Yellow Tavern" several regiments of our cavalry (mine among them) were dismounted, formed across the fields, and moved forward in real line of battle style until we came upon the enemy, also dismounted. After a brisk encounter we fell back to a road that was somewhat sunken.

There we halted for the purpose of stopping the enemy's advance, for the sunken road furnished us some protection, but they did not stop. They marched on, firing as they came.

Their line was longer and thicker than ours, and it was evident that we were about to be surrounded. Some of our men mounted the fence in the rear and fled across the fields. Others stood their ground and were captured, I among them.

I was near Colonel Pate, the colonel commanding a regiment in my brigade. He was killed by a bullet striking him in the centre of the forehead. Also near me was our captain, Bruce Gibson.

There was a little culvert across a ditch in the road that the farmers used in going from the road into the field. Some of our men crept under this culvert and escaped. Probably 200 of us were captured.

But the army sustained a greater loss than that, a loss second only to that of Stonewall Jackson.

Just behind our line in the field was Gen. Stuart with his

staff. A bullet struck him somewhere about the stomach. He was held on his horse until it was led to a place of safety. Then he was taken from his horse, put into an ambulance and carried to Richmond. He died the next day.

Stuart was considered the greatest cavalry leader of the war on either side, and his death brought a very great loss to Gen. Lee, and also to the whole Confederacy.

The Confederacy had from the beginning attached greater importance to the cavalry arm of the service than had the North, and many had been the daring raids that Stuart made within the enemy's lines, capturing thousands of wagons laden with military stores, and many thousand prisoners. In fact, almost our entire cavalry was equipped with saddles, bridles and arms captured from the enemy; nearly all the wagons in Lee's army were captured wagons. But perhaps Providence knew that the time was near at hand when we would not need these things, so He permitted the one who had been the means of supplying our wants in this particular to retire from the field. He was buried in Hollywood Cemetery, Richmond, Va., and a magnificent equestrian statue marks the spot.

Many of Stuart's raids were made under the cover of darkness. He always wore a long ostrich feather in his hat, and was a splendid rider. The soldiers had a war song, the chorus of which was something like this: "*We'll follow the feather of Stuart tonight.*"

The prisoners were taken back and put under guard. I think this was about 4 o'clock in the afternoon. We remained there quietly until after dark, all the time, however, the fighting was going on, but we were out of reach of danger in that respect, so we had a brief breathing spell.

After dark Sheridan's whole command began to move slowly toward Richmond, making frequent stops of a few minutes. The prisoners marched two abreast, with a line of cavalry guard on each side. We had, of course, to keep up with the cavalry.

Our guard was very kind to us, and allowed us to take hold of their stirrup straps, which was quite a help to us as we marched along, especially in crossing streams, one of which I remember

A battle-scarred Confederate banner.

was up to our waists. It began raining at midnight, and continued most of the next day. The night was very dark, and from the distance we had covered from the time we started, it seemed to us that we must be very near the city. Finally we turned to the left and moved toward the James River, in a south-easterly direction from Richmond.

As we had no sleep the night before, but rode all night, and now were walking all night in the rain and mud, and without food, you may know we were in a wretched condition. Every now and then a friendly Yank would hand us a cracker from his haversack, saying, "Here, Johnnie." But they were on short rations themselves, and could not help us much in that respect.

The next day we were in constant peril from the shells thrown from the Confederate batteries, that seemed to come in every direction. In fact, Sheridan was completely surrounded, except on one side, and his progress was stopped there by the Chickahominy River.

This is a slow, marshy river, crossed by two or three bridges. The chief one had been destroyed by the Confederates. Sheridan was in close quarters, and we prisoners had made up our minds that he would have to surrender his army.

We got so bold and impudent that we hailed Yankee officers as they passed us, and said, "Hey there, Mr. Yank, I speak for that horse."

Among these officers so hailed was a red-headed major, who was in command of our guard. Prior to this, he had been very surly and exceedingly gruff and harsh. So much so, that the prisoners had whispered among themselves that if we did get him in our hands we'd make him sweat, and when it became evident not only to us, but to the enemy, that they were in danger of capture, this particular officer changed his attitude toward us very perceptibly. He took our jeers and taunts without a word, and, luckily for us, about this time he was relieved of his position, and another put in his place. Perhaps he had asked for it, knowing that he wouldn't receive very kind treatment if he fell into our hands.

But, oh, the irony of Fate. On a hill fronting the river (not far from the bridge) was an old Virginia mansion. The prisoners were led to this house and ordered to tear it down and carry the timbers to the river and rebuild the bridge. What do you think of that? Of course, we had to obey, but we made loud complaints, and while we were carrying this timber and rebuilding the bridge, our enemy was protecting us, from their standpoint (as far as they could), by keeping back the Confederates, who were pouring shot and shell into their ranks from every direction. The bridge was repaired, Sheridan's command was soon safe on the other side, and our hopes died away.

There are two little incidents connected with my capture that I ought not to leave out, so I will go back to that event. The first one may serve a good purpose if the reader is ever placed in similar circumstances.

When I realized that we were in the hands of the enemy, but before they had gotten to where I was, I lay down on my face in the ditch alongside of the wounded and dead, pretending myself to be dead. I had the most awful feeling while lying there imaginable, and felt that at any moment I might be thrust through with a bayonet, and the feeling was so intense that as soon as I heard the Yankees tramping about me and calling upon the men to surrender, I got up and surrendered. If I had only had presence of mind enough to have lain on my back and watched them from the corner of my eye, I might have passed through the ordeal and escaped after they left, as they did not remain long.

In the first place, the men were cavalrymen, and hence had no bayonets. Then again, the Confederate bullets were hissing about their ears in such a manner that they never would have thought of testing a "Johnnie Reb" in that way in order to see whether he was really dead or playing possum.

The other incident was the second night after our capture. It was still raining, and the weather was quite cool for the season (it was about the 10th of May). We were all wet to the skin, and nearly starved. We were stopped in a field, a guard placed around us, an old cow driven up and shot, and we were told to help ourselves. So every fellow that could get a knife went up and cut his own steak. They gave us some fence rails, out of which we made little fires and broiled our cow meat. She may have been tough and old, and I know we had no salt, but the meat was as sweet to us as any porterhouse steak we had ever eaten.

We huddled together for the night like pigs, and slept comfortably, notwithstanding we had tramped the earth into a mud hole.

But to go back to the crossing of the Chickahominy River. Once across that river, the enemy seemed to have very little opposition to their march toward the James.

I know it was a long, weary march, and their horses were giving out all along the way. When a horse got too sore-footed to travel, he was shot, and as we passed along we saw hundreds of these horses, with the warm life-blood flowing from a hole in their foreheads, lying by the side of the road. This was done to prevent the horses from falling into the hands of the Confederates.

When we got in sight of the James River, the prisoners were halted in an orchard, and rested there for an hour or so. Just over the fence were some little pigs, with their tails curled around like a curl on a girl's head, rooting around for something nice to eat. One of the prisoners called to a Yankee to catch a pig and throw it over the fence. He at once made a dive for the pigs and got one, and threw it to us. A great crowd rushed for the pig, every fellow with a knife in his hand, and as many as could get hold of the little fellow began cutting into his anatomy. I had hold of one of the hind legs, and while we cut, the pig squealed. I got a whole ham for my share. Of course, I shared it with my comrades.

We gathered sticks and built little fires, and had a grand feast of roast pig. My, it was sweet! There was neither ceremony, pepper nor salt.

Soon after this banquet we were marched to the James River, put on a steamer, and our empty stomachs filled to the brim with a good dinner. The first course was good beef soup, thickened with vegetables. We certainly enjoyed it. Then came roast beef and real baker's bread (something we hadn't had for an age).

But to go back to Spotsylvania Courthouse. Grant's efforts to get to Richmond by breaking through Lee's lines were as ineffectual there as they had been in the Wilderness two days before. So he packed his grip (so to speak) and made another move toward the James River.

These two battles, of course, had reduced his fighting forces materially, but the Government at Washington kept filling up his ranks and supplying him with every need. In fact, in one case particularly, they sent him more war material than he could use, and rather than encumber his march, he sent 100 cannon back to Washington, while the poor Confeds had no such source of supply, and had to be content with making the best of the material they had.

Gen. Lee moved his army in a parallel line with Grant's, and kept in his front, ready to dispute his passage if he attempted to move forward.

CHAPTER 9

From James River to Petersburg

Down on the left of the Rebel lines,
Where a breastwork stands on a copse of pines,
Before the Rebels their ranks can form,
The Yankees have carried the place by storm.

I think it was about the 12th of May when Grant began his march from Spotsylvania, and it was, I think, the 3rd of June when he made another attempt at Cold Harbor to enter Richmond by breaking through Lee's army, and another desperate battle was fought, but the losses were not so great as they were at the Wilderness or Spotsylvania. Grant, however, was again defeated, and continued his march toward the James River. In this battle the colonel of my regiment (Flournoy) was killed. He was a dashing young colonel, but not as prudent as an officer should be. At the time he was killed he was standing on the top of the breastworks, behind which men were fighting, shouting defiance at the enemy, and challenging them to come out in the open and fight it out. Of course, it did not take them long to put a bullet through his body. At one time he was major of the regiment, then lieutenant-colonel, and on the retirement of his father, he was made colonel. His father was once Governor of the State. Richards, Captain of Company C, was made colonel of our regiment, and held this position during the war. He had commanded a company of cavalry from Clark county, Virginia.

Grant differed from other commanders who fought the army of Northern Virginia in this respect—he refused to acknowledge defeat. If his attacks failed at one point after repeated attempts, he would move his army to the left and attack again. This he kept up to the end of the war.

Not being able to reach Richmond by attacking Lee on the north side of the river, he crossed his main army to the south side, and stretching out his line of battle from the James to Petersburg, began a long siege, that lasted through the fall and winter till late in the spring.

Now to go back to prison.

The steamer on which we were placed and given such a good, substantial dinner, soon after this took its departure down the James and landed us at Fortress Monroe, where we were put in an inclosure with a number of other prisoners, and among them the officers and crew of the British steamer *Grayhound*, that had been captured while trying to run a blockade into one of the Southern ports.

They all seemed to be Southern sympathizers, and whenever they had an opportunity showed the Confederate prisoners much kindness, even going so far as to distribute gold among them, of which they seemed to have an abundant supply. This was, of course, done on the sly, and the Confederates were careful to conceal these gifts. Those who were well enough off to wear stockings, slipped the gold in their stocking-leg. Some put it in their mouths. This was necessary, as the prisoners were frequently searched.

These Englishmen were loud in their protests, and were making all kinds of threats as to what their Government would do if it learned of their treatment.

After remaining there a few days the Confederates were again marched aboard a steamer and taken to "Point Lookout," where a regular prison-camp had been established. I think there were about 15,000 prisoners at this camp guarded by negro troops, which made our Southern blood boil. As the darkies used to say, "The bottom rail had got on top."

The camp was on a point of land formed by the junction of the Potomac River and Chesapeake Bay on the north side of the river. I imagine there were about ten acres of ground, surrounded by a high board fence, probably about 14 feet high. Just below the top was built a platform about three feet wide, and on this platform the guards walked to and fro with their guns on their shoulders. From their position they could overlook the whole camp, as the ground was perfectly level. There was also a strong guard inside the camp, while artillery and regiments of infantry were stationed near the camp to guard it from outside attack, and one or more gunboats patrolled the waters that nearly surrounded the camp.

Notwithstanding this precaution, occasionally prisoners made their escape. One ingenious method that baffled our guards for a long time was the following:

The prisoners were allowed to go outside of the enclosure on the beach to bathe. And if an empty barrel or box happened to be floating on the water, a prisoner in bathing would watch his opportunity, slip his head under the barrel or box, and then as the tide drifted up the river, would follow it, keeping as near the shore as necessary until he got beyond the reach of the guard, and then take to the woods.

The punishment for trying to escape was cruel. Those who were caught at it were strung up to a pole by the thumbs, with the tips of their toes just touching the ground. Sometimes the men would faint, and had to be cut down.

Upon the whole, prison life was very monotonous. It was an unhealthy camp; so much so, that the prisoners considered that they had a better chance for their lives fighting in the army.

The water was brackish and unpleasant to the taste. The only water we had was from pumps scattered about over the camps, and during the four months that I was there the pumps were always surrounded by a thirsty crowd of from 40 to 50 prisoners, each with his tin-cup, trying to wedge his way in, that he might quench his thirst.

The food, while good, was very scant. Breakfast consisted of coffee and a loaf of bread, which, under ordinary circumstances, with vegetables and other food, would probably suffice for two meals. This loaf was given us at breakfast, and if we ate it all then we went without bread for dinner. If there was any left over we took it to our tents, laid it on the ground, and saved it for dinner.

The dinners consisted of a tin-cup of soup (generally bean or other vegetable), a small piece of meat on a tinplate, on which a little vinegar was poured to prevent scurvy. My recollection is we had no other meal, but my mind is not perfectly clear on this point. I do know, however, that we were always hungry, and the chief topic of conversation was the sumptuous meals we had sat down to in other days.

As I recalled the tables of former years laden with bacon, cabbage, potatoes and hominy, I remember how I reproached myself for not having eaten more when I had the opportunity. Delicacies never entered into the discussion; it was always the plain, simple foods that we talked about and longed for.

We were told that the short rations were given us in retaliation for the scanty food supplied to their soldiers in Southern prisons.

The hospitals were crowded all the time, and there were many sick in the camp waiting their opportunity to go into hospitals.

We lived in what is known as Sibley tents, shaped like a bell, with an opening in the top about 15 inches in diameter.

There were 12 men to a tent, who, when they slept, arranged themselves in a circle, like the spokes of a wagon, with their feet toward the centre. These tents were as close as they could stand on the ground, with wide avenues between every two rows of tents, thus allowing every tent to front on an avenue.

Every day the prisoners were called out of their tents and formed in line; roll was called and the prisoners searched. And while they were being searched, the guards were searching the tents. For just what purpose this search was done I do not know, unless it was for fear that arms might be smuggled in to be used by the prisoners for making their escape.

Many of the prisoners had a peculiar affection of the eyes, caused, perhaps, by the glare from the white tents, the sand, and the reflection from the water. There was nothing green to be seen anywhere, consequently many of the prisoners became blind for a portion of the 24 hours. Just as the sun was sinking behind the fence they would become totally blind, and had to be led about by someone. As morning light came the blindness would disappear.

Some of the prisoners who were mechanics or artisans got work outside, but I believe they got no pay except full rations and the privilege of bringing things into camp, such as blocks of wood, pieces of metal, etc. Out of these were manufactured a great many interesting little articles—small steam locomotives, wooden fans, rings from rubber buttons set with gold and silver, and sometimes gems. One ingenious fellow built a small distillery and made whiskey from potato rinds or whatever refuse he could pick up, and got drunk on the product.

All about the camp were boards on which these manufactured articles were exposed for sale. A cracker would buy a chew of tobacco. The tobacco was cut up into chews and half chews. The crackers were brought in by the men who went out to work. I cannot recall all the curious things that were exposed for sale within the camp.

Whilst in prison, twice I was very kindly remembered by Miss Melissa Baker of Baltimore, Md., who sent me boxes containing provisions, clothing, towels, soap, toothbrush, jars of preserves, cooked ham, crackers, lemons, tea, coffee and sugar. When I received the first box I just concluded that I was going to kill myself eating. I ate, and ate, and ate. I simply could not stop; and so did all my comrades in the tent.

So, of course, the box didn't last long. However, at first I suffered no evil consequences, but finally, like most of the other prisoners, was taken sick (but not from eating), and my comrades made application for my entrance into the hospital. I had to wait a week or ten days before there was a vacancy. I was carried there on a stretcher, and was so sick that I had to be fed.

Soon after my entrance into the hospital Caleb Rector was brought in. His home was on the turnpike between Middleburg and Upperville. He had a scorching fever, and was soon delirious. I put my hand on him, and the heat almost burned me. One day a nurse took a wet towel and put it on his forehead. Although he was unconscious, I saw a smile play over his face, and as the nurse was bending over him he reached up one hand and caught the nurse by the hair; then pulling his head down, and lifting the wet towel with his other hand, tried to put it on the nurse's forehead. That act revealed the character of the man. He was open-hearted and generous, and the cool towel on his forehead was so pleasant to him that he wanted the nurse to share it with him.

The nurses were all men, chosen from among the prisoners. I never saw a woman the whole time I was in prison.

The hospitals were long tents, each holding about 30 cots. As soon as a patient died, he was taken out to the dead-house, the sheets changed, and another brought in.

When I was first taken there I remarked to my neighbour that I did not think that was very healthy (meaning the placing of a new patient at once on a bed that was still warm from the body that had just been removed). He replied that the bed that I was on had been occupied by a smallpox patient, and I was put on it a few minutes after the patient was taken out.

However, there was a separate hospital for contagious diseases, and the patient was removed as soon as the disease developed.

Most of those who went into the hospital died. The dead were all carried at once to the dead-house on stretchers, and once a day a two-horse wagon came in, and their bodies were laid in it like so much cord wood, uncoffined, taken out and buried in long trenches. The trenches were seven feet wide and three feet deep, and the bodies were laid across the trench side by side and covered with earth.

I had been in prison about four months when news came that the two Governments had agreed upon an exchange of prisoners; it only included the sick in the hospitals. Of course, every patient in the hospital was on the anxious bench and wondering whether he would be included among the fortunate ones. Some

GEN. A.P. HILL,
Commanding a corps of Lee's army.
Killed just before the final surrender.

days afterward a corps of physicians came to the hospital tents examining the different patients that lay in the cots, taking the name of one and leaving another. I happened to be among those who were selected for exchange. The object seemed to be to take only those who were not liable to be fit for service soon.

We were not at this time exchanged, but each side had agreed to parole the sick from the hospitals, that is, those who were not too ill to be moved. At one time the two Governments freely exchanged prisoners, but this worked so much to the advantage of the South that the North refused to continue the agreement. All Southern soldiers were enlisted for the war, and when the prisoners came back from the North they went at once into the armies of the Confederacy, while Northern prisoners, returning from the South, mostly went to their homes, as they enlisted for one year, and their terms of service in most cases had about expired.

Then again, the South was taxed severely to feed its own soldiers and citizens, and were only too glad to get rid of the burden of caring for Northern prisoners, and hence the North did all they could to restrict the exchange of prisoners, but there was such a pressure brought to bear upon the U.S. Government by those who had sick and wounded friends confined in Southern prisons, that now and then each side would parole a number of prisoners from the hospitals who might later be exchanged. My recollection is that about 1500 Confederate prisoners in the hospital at Point Lookout were paroled at this time, and I among them.

We were put on a steamer and carried to a point below Richmond, on the James River, where we met a like number of Federal prisoners that came down from Richmond, and there the exchange was made. The vessel that carried us up the river was a small one, and the sick were packed on the deck and in the hold of the vessel as thick as they could lay. They were all sick, but had to lie on the hard decks with no attention, except that a doctor now and then went through the vessel handing out pills to any who wanted them. He carried them loose in his pocket, and as he stepped between and over the men as they lay on the hard beds, he would say, "Who wants a pill?" And all around him the bony, emaciated arms would be stretched up to receive the medicine. What the pills contained no one knew, but the suffering men swallowed them and asked no questions. They were sick, and needed medicine, and this was medicine. What more did a sick soldier need? The disease, however, was almost entirely a bowel affection, and, perhaps, the same medicine served for all cases. Many died on the way. A large number of the dead were put off at Fortress Monroe as the vessel passed.

Just before reaching the point where the vessels were to meet in the river, our vessel was drawn up alongside of a fine large steamer, and we were transferred to it.

All the very sick were placed upon new mattresses. This was the condition in which we were received by our Confederate friends.

The vessel that landed us on the bank of the James took back the Federal prisoners that had been brought down from Richmond, but I hardly think they were transferred to the smaller vessel that brought us from Point Lookout. The Federal authorities were ashamed to let the officers of the Confederate Government see the miserable condition in which we were transported; hence the transfer to the larger vessel just before delivering us to the Confederates. As soon as we landed we were all given a tincup of hot, nutritious soup, the like of which we had not tasted since leaving our homes for the field, unless it was the soup the Yanks had given us four months before when we embarked on the James river for Fortress Monroe prison.

We were conveyed from this point to Richmond by rail, and distributed among the various army hospitals in the city. I was sent to the Chimborazo Hospital, on the outskirts of the city, located on a bluff looking down the river, within hearing distance of the siege guns on Dury's Bluff, on the James. These were constantly throwing missiles of some sort at the Yankee gunboats below. I remained in the hospital about ten days, and then was considered well enough to go into camp with other convalescents. There were several hundred of us. The camp was near the city.

Some were paroled prisoners and some were from the hospitals of the city, but not strong enough to return to their commands.

All who could reach their homes were allowed leave of absence, but much of the Confederate territory was then in the hands of the Northern armies, and all whose homes could not in safety be reached were placed in camps until they were in condition for active service. Of course, those on parole could not re-enter the army until regularly exchanged.

After remaining in this camp a short time and receiving in Confederate paper money a portion of our pay, we were marched into Richmond and to one of the depots. We did not know what disposition they intended making of us (perhaps we were going to a new camp), but there was a train that was just starting out for Gordonsville, so three of us got on the rear platform of the end car and thus beat our way to Gordonsville without being noticed. This was as far as the train could go in safety on account of the proximity of the enemy. When we got off we noticed Gen. Lee standing in the crowd, having just alighted from the train. I had often seen him, but never got as close to him as I desired. Now, this was my chance. I went up within five feet of him, and took a good look.

I never expect again to look upon such a splendid piece of humanity. He was dressed in a new Confederate uniform that fitted him perfectly, with long-legged boots, reaching above the knees. His collar was adorned on each side with three gold stars, surrounded by a gold wreath. His head was covered with a new soft black hat, encircled with a gold cord, from which dangled two gold acorns, one on each end. His hands were covered with yellow buckskin gauntlets, reaching one-third the way to his elbows. His beard was iron-gray, white predominating; it was closely clipped, and was what is called a full beard. I imagined that he was a little over six feet and would weigh 190 pounds. His eyes, I think, were brown, and as bright as stars. No picture could possibly do him justice. I suppose it would take cycles of time to produce another such as he—so perfect in form and feature.

We three at once struck off across the fields to go as far as we could toward our homes. We moved in the direction of Charlottesville, and, avoiding the town, passed beyond, but were soon apprised of the fact that we could not go farther without danger of running into the enemy. We put up at a farmhouse for a few days, and after learning that the enemy had withdrawn from the immediate vicinity, we took to the road, our destination being the home of my brother Gerard, a farmer living near McGaheysville, Rockingham County, just west of the Blue Ridge. We arrived there in due time, and remained quite a while, perhaps a month. We did work about the farm, which was accepted as compensation for our board. Of course, no one thought of asking money consideration from a soldier, and as far as I was concerned, I felt free to come and go without money and without price.

When I was captured I rode a borrowed horse, belonging to one of the members of my command. This horse was not captured with me, and was taken possession of by the owner, but I had a horse that I had left with my brother Gerard to recuperate, and when I reached there I expected to use this horse in getting home. Imagine my disappointment when I was told that he was dead. His rest and good pasture had put fresh blood in his veins and vigorous life in his body, and one day, as he was sporting in the field and performing various gymnastic stunts, he broke a blood vessel, and bled to death.

My brother John, who was then in prison, had a horse there also. I pressed that horse into service, and started for home late in the fall. I got safely through the enemy's lines, and received a warm welcome by the folks at home. I was still a paroled prisoner, and had to refrain from going on any of the expeditions that were making Mosby and his men famous and a terror to the authorities in Washington, although I was strongly tempted to do so. The winter was spent pretty much as the one I have already described. The life of the Confederacy, for whose existence we had suffered and lost so much, was hanging in the balance. Every family was mourning the loss of one or more dead or maimed; food and clothing could hardly be obtained at any price. To add to the distressed condition, a decree had gone out from Washington that all the mills, barns, provender for beast and food for man was to be burned, and all cattle and horses of every description found, driven off. This decree had been carried out with a cruelty that in the light of present-day civilization seems incredible.

The armies, *like the locust of Egypt*, went out from Washington, swept down the rich valley of Virginia beyond Staunton and destroyed or carried off everything except the homes and the old men and women and children who occupied them. Many of these homes were destroyed by catching fire from the burning barns and mills. Every part of Virginia within reach of the Northern armies suffered the same devastation.

While I write this, a gentleman sits in my office who was in the Northern army and took part in the burning. I have just read the foregoing to him and asked him if it were not true. "Yes," said he, "every word of it."

Notwithstanding this condition of things, everywhere might be heard the cry, "On with the dance, let joy be unconfined." Mosby's fame as a daring raider had spread far and wide, and his command had increased to over 500. Dashing young cavaliers from every part of Virginia, mounted upon handsome steeds, came trooping in to join his command. They were mostly boys who were too young to enter the army at the beginning of hostilities, but now, as they became old enough to be ranked as soldiers, were anxious to get into the midst of the greatest excitement. The hills and valleys of Loudoun and Fauquier, coupled with parts of the adjacent counties, furnished the field, and John S. Mosby of Warrenton, Va., was accepted as their leader.

What might we expect when these 500 handsome young men, all well mounted and armed, in whose veins flowed the blood of the heroes of the revolution? These 500 heroes, coming in every few days, some of them with the marks of the battle on their bodies and trophies of victories in their hands. What do you suppose those Virginia girls were going to do about it, put on sackcloth and ashes? Well, it was sackcloth they wore, and many of their treasures were in ashes, but their spirits were unbroken. They had faith in the God of battles, and while they could not bear arms, they said, "Let us make merry, for these are our brothers and lovers; we should cheer them with laughter and song; it will make them stronger and braver." And so it did, and they fiddled and danced while "*Rome burned*."

Sometime during the latter part of the winter I learned that all the prisoners who were paroled at a certain time had been exchanged, and were ordered to rejoin their various commands. That included me.

As I was no longer under obligation not to take up arms against the U.S. Government, I could not refrain from taking some part in the upholding of what was often called Mosby's Confederacy (meaning the territory in which he operated), so I was tempted to steal a few more days before obeying the order from Richmond. I went with Mosby on one occasion when the Yankees made a raid through Loudoun and Fauquier with cavalry and artillery seeking to annihilate his command. Mosby had all his force out on the occasion, and hung on the enemy's front flanks and rear from the time they entered Mosby's territory until they left. He did not allow them time to eat, sleep or rest. In an encounter near my home a Yankee's horse was killed, from which I took the bridle, which was a very fine one. In doing so I got my hands bloody, and the blood from the bridle stained my clothes. This started the rumour that I was wounded, and it reached my home before I got there, but I soon arrived and explained the mistake.

Shortly afterward I was in company with a number of others *en route* for Lee's army, the greater portion of which was south of Richmond, stretching from there to Petersburg.

Now to go back to my capture at Yellow Tavern. After Grant's repulse at Cold Harbor he crossed the James River with his army and began the siege of Richmond, which lasted all through the remainder of the fall and winter of 1864 and 1865 into April.

The colonel of my regiment (Flournoy), who I stated was killed at the Battle of Cold Harbor, was the last of the colonels in my brigade to lose his life. A gallant young officer, but a little too fond of the bottle, not very choice in his language, rather reckless. A few days before he was killed he remarked to one of his staff as they stood around the camp-fire, "I don't believe the bullet that is to kill me has yet been moulded." Foolish man; at that very time, not far from where he stood, was a soldier in blue carrying about his waist a leather cartridge-box that held the very bullet that was to end his life, and not many hours afterward that bullet and that colonel met. The latter surrendered without a word.

The winter was a long, dreary one, and the Confederates, being compelled to live in the trenches night and day, suffered terribly from cold and hunger. Wade Hampton took Gen. Stuart's place after the latter's death, and during the winter made a raid inside Grant's lines and drove out 1500 head of fat cattle. It did not take Lee's hungry soldiers long to dispose of them and lick their chops for more. Grant's great army, stretching from the James river to Petersburg, compelled Gen. Lee to do the same with his little, half-starved and scantily-clothed force, and all winter long Grant pounded away at Lee's front, trying to break through.

The most sensational event that occurred was the Battle of the Crater, as it was called. Grant attempted to break Lee's line by digging a great tunnel, which had for its object the blowing up of Lee's intrenchments, and then in the confusion, rushing a large force into the opening. The tunnel was finished up to and under Lee's line and loaded with explosives. I believe there was a premature explosion, which resulted in the killing of more of Grant's soldiers than of Lee's, and then the attack that followed resulted in a great slaughter of Grant's men and the total failure of the project.

CHAPTER 10

From Petersburg to Appomattox and Home

There hangs a sabre, and there a rein,
With a rusty buckle and a green curb chain;
A pair of spurs on the old grey wall,
And a mouldy saddle—well, that is all.

April 2, 1865, Lee was compelled to evacuate Richmond, abandon his whole battle line, and fall back toward the mountains. He hoped to be able to join his forces with those of Gen. Jos. E. Johnston, who was advancing northward through North Carolina, but his losses were so heavy and his army almost starved, the road deep with mud from excessive rains, making it impossible for his gaunt, lean horses to draw his artillery and wagons. He saw further resistance was useless, so on April 9, 1865, Lee surrendered what was left of his once formidable army. The number was a little less than 8000 men. I have seen it stated that Lee had about 35,000 men,[1] when, on April 2, he ordered the evacuation of his line of intrenchments. Some of his cavalry, being on the outskirts, were not included in the surrender.

Besides this, during the seven days' retreat, Grant's forces were

---

1. General Longstreet says the total number surrendered to Grant was 28,356. Many of these came in voluntarily and surrendered. Lee had with him 1500 prisoners, taken since leaving Petersburg. These were the first to be delivered to the Union army. The first generous act Grant did after the surrender was to furnish Lee's hungry soldiers and horses with food. Grant's army must have numbered not far from 150,000.

ONE OF STONEWALL JACKSON'S MILEPOSTS. A FAMILIAR SIGHT TO THOSE WHO TRAVELED THE VALLEY TURNPIKE DURING THE CIVIL WAR.

pressing Lee's army on all sides, killing, wounding and capturing some of his men every hour; this accounts for the small number that Gen. Lee personally surrendered. The first thing that was done after the surrender was an application from Gen. Lee to Grant for food for his horses and men, which was promptly supplied. Of course, there is much that is interesting in connection with the surrender that need not be recorded here. Grant's treatment of Lee and his soldiers won for him praise all over the South.

But to go back. As I have said, I was on the march from home toward the army, and had reached a point not far from Charlottesville. There were about a dozen of us, all belonging to my regiment. About noon we saw advancing toward us a small body of cavalry. At first we took them for the enemy and approached them cautiously, they using the same precaution. When we discovered that we were fellow-Confeds we passed with a salute. One of them called to us and said, "Boys, you may as well go home; Lee has surrendered his army." We paid no attention to it, but moved on. A mile farther we met another squad and asked what was the news from the army. We got this reply: "As we passed through Charlottesville we came near being mobbed for telling the news from the army. You had better go on and find out for yourselves."

Soon after this we met a colonel leading about 40 cavalrymen. By this time we began to feel that something was wrong. The colonel halted his men and frankly told us that it was a fact that Lee had surrendered his army. He stated that some of the cavalry had escaped and they were making their way toward their homes, and advised us to do the same. The colonel and his men moved on, and we halted for an hour in the road discussing the situation and trying to determine what to do. We were not prepared to act upon the evidence that we had had regarding the surrender, but were willing to admit that it might be true. One fellow from Company F, riding a gray horse, rose in his stirrups, and lifting his clinched hand high above his head, said, "If Gen. Lee has had to surrender his army, there is not a just God in

Heaven."

Finally we decided to cross the mountains into the Virginia Valley and tarry in the vicinity of Staunton and await further tidings. I made a bee-line for my brother Gerard's. The others scattered here and there. After remaining a few days at my brother's I started, in company with six or eight others, who were from the lower end of the valley, principally Clark county, for my home in Loudoun, with no definite idea as to what I should do before I got there. In fact, the others were in the same frame of mind.

We had heard and read the proclamation that all Confederate soldiers who would surrender their arms and take the oath of allegiance to the U.S. Government (except a certain grade of officers) would be allowed to go to their homes and not be molested, but we had not yet come to the point of surrendering.

We moved on down the valley pike, noting as we went the terrible havoc the war had made, commenting on what we called Jackson's mileposts, *viz.* the skeletons of horses that had fallen by the way. They were, however, too thick to be called mileposts, but that is what we called them.

A little below Woodstock, I think it was, we saw on a hill, standing in the middle of the road facing us, two sentinels on horseback. They were Yankee pickets. I think there were eight of us. We halted. Someone said, "Well, boys, what are we going to do? We can't pass these pickets. Shall we surrender?" I guess we stood there for an hour. We were all mounted.

Finally a young fellow from Clark county said, "I'm going up and surrender."

Another said, "I go with you."

And the two, taking something in their hands that would pass for a flag of truce (white handkerchiefs had become obsolete), went forward and were allowed to pass. They went to headquarters and surrendered. Then one by one the little band melted away, leaving two, and I was one of them. We were not ready to surrender. We went back out of sight, and made a flank movement to get into the foothills of the Massanutten mountains, and by keeping under cover of the timber, managed to get within 12 miles of my home without being molested.

As we stood on the edge of the woods we saw the Yankee cavalry moving up and down the turnpike running from Paris to Middleburg. It looked as if there was nothing else to do but surrender. At this point my comrade deserted me and went forward and surrendered. I watched my opportunity, slipping across the pike unobserved, and following the Blue Ridge mountains until nearly opposite my home, took a straight line across the fields and reached home safely. As I carried my full complement of arms I created no little surprise and consternation.

Union soldiers were constantly passing along the road which ran close by my home, some of them stopping for water or for information, but I could not fully make up my mind to surrender. My brother Richard of Mosby's command was of the same mind. Mosby and all his men had surrendered, and the family pleaded with us to do the same, but we were obstinate. This, however, was nothing to our credit. When one is whipped he should be man enough to acknowledge it and brave enough to surrender, unless the conqueror be a cannibal.

Thus ended my career as a soldier. As I look back over those four eventful years, after a lapse of over 40 years, (as at time of first publication), it all seems a dream. In time of peace it is a struggle for 75 *per cent.* of us to get a fair living out of the earth, but the people down South managed to live, and were in a degree comfortable and contented, and managed to get food enough to preserve their bodies and keep them strong and healthy. Flour was $500 a barrel. I paid $125 in Richmond for a hat that I could now buy for $1. This common red-striped candy, $25 per pound. Samuel Rector had gone from Loudoun county to Richmond in 1864 on some business.

When ready to go home he thought it would be nice and the proper thing to do to take the family some little remembrances. He went into a confectionery store and asked to see some candies. The jars were taken down and he tasted first one then another. Selecting one and asking the price, he was told that it was

$25 per pound. It was of the long, red-striped variety just mentioned, worth in times of peace about 10 cents per pound. He had a pound of it wrapped up, and handed the proprietor a $50 Confederate note. Twenty dollars was handed back in change. Mr. Rector said, "I understood you to say the price was $25."

"That is true," said the affable confectioner, "but you ate $5 worth."

The joke was well worth $5 to Mr. Rector, and he got more pleasure out of it than he did out of the pound of candy.

There were four commodities with which the South was plentifully supplied, *viz.*, tobacco, cotton, money and horses. We raised the two former in the territory not harassed by marching armies. The third was supplied by printing presses, and the horses were captured from our enemy. Of course, bridles, saddles, harness and wagons came with the horses.

I have omitted a great many little entertaining incidents partly for the sake of brevity and partly because they escaped my memory at the time they should have been narrated. One that I just now recall, and one which the children always used to make me tell whenever war stories were called for, regardless of how often it had been repeated, I will insert here:

One cold, windy night in the winter of '62 I was on picket on the turnpike between Upperville and Middleburg. Pickets in the Confederate army always stood alone, as two or more would likely be absorbed in conversation and forget their duty. We were also admonished not to dismount. I was a little reckless that night, and dismounting stood leaning against my horse to break the bleak wind and absorb as much heat from his body as possible. He became restless, and I noticed that he was looking intently down the pike and throwing his head up and down as horses will do when excited.

I listened, but could hear no sound, and told my steed to keep still, but his keen eyes or ears saw or heard something that worried him, and he kept his ears pointed down in the direction from which the enemy would probably come if they came at all. I said to myself, "You had better mount your horse." But I delayed. I then recalled the fact that news had reached the camp that day that a body of cavalry had left the vicinity of Washington and was moving northeast, and we were admonished to keep a sharp lookout. Then I concluded to mount, but before I could do so I realized that it was too late.

I was standing close by one of those old Virginia stone fences, about five feet high, and in the darkness I saw an object creeping up on the other side of the fence, close to it, and only a few feet from where I stood. I immediately concluded that the object was a man, and that he was from the enemy and was bent on capturing or killing the picket, so as to surprise our camp. The most accessible weapon I had was my sabre. I drew it and made a cut at what I conceived to be the man's head. As I did so, the object disappeared behind the fence, and in its place appeared what proved to be a black cat's tail, which in a flash followed the cat. Although it was quite dark, the little black object appearing between me and the sky was plainly visible. This incident taught me a lesson that I never forgot. I mounted my horse, and never was known afterward to dismount when on the picket line. I believe this was the greatest fright I encountered during my whole four years' war experience.

One more little incident, and a short tribute to the remarkable fidelity of the coloured people of the South to the Southern cause and the families of their owners, and I shall have finished.

There was in my company a soldier by the name of Owens— Mason Owens. He was a splendid fellow, quiet in his demeanour, brave in battle, always in his place, whether that place was in the front or rear rank, but never liked to do anything that called for disguise or deception, such as acting as a spy or disguised as a Union soldier, in order to get into the enemy's camp, although he recognized that it was necessary to have men for work of this kind. Owens was very fond of me; in fact, I had no more faithful friend in the army. He was continually with me, doing me favors, sharing with me any delicacy that came into his possession, keeping close by me in battle.

Sometimes when the regiment would be ordered to dismount

for the purpose of engaging the foe on foot (and he was No. 4, making it his duty to remain mounted and take care of Nos. 1, 2, and 3 horses), he would quickly dismount and take my place in the ranks and leave me the care of the horses (a place few objected to having), and many like favours. One afternoon, near night, our captain said that he had a requisition for six picked men to do some hazardous night-work within the enemy's lines, just the kind of duty that Owens detested. But fate was against him, and he and five others were selected. He sullenly complied, and as he rode out of the ranks with his face flushed and his head bowed, I heard him say, "I don't like this."

Someone said, "Owens, I'll take your place."

He turned and gave him a look that must have chilled the fellow's blood, and said, "*Didn't you hear Capt. Gibson call me?*"

I saw the six ride off; Owens didn't even say goodbye to me. That night one of Lee's noted scouts led these men, with others taken from other commands, into the enemy's camp, and Owens never returned. He was shot, and fell from his horse, dying either from cold or the wound. At intervals during the night a citizen living near where he fell heard someone calling, but was afraid to go out. The next morning he found his dead body and buried it. I grieved very much over his death, occurring as it did.

Now I want to say that I shall ever have a tender spot in my breast for the coloured people, owing to what I know of the race, judged from my association with them from early childhood up to and including the years of the Civil War, and, indeed, some years after.

My home in Loudoun County, on the border line between the North and South, gave me an unusual opportunity of judging how far the negro could be trusted in caring for and protecting the homes of the men who were in the Southern armies. Scattered all through the South, and especially in the border States, there were white men who were not in sympathy with the South, and some of them acted as spies and guides for the Northern troops as they marched and counter-marched through the land. But I never knew of a negro being guilty of like conduct. They not only watched over and protected the women and children in their homes, but were equally as faithful and careful to protect the Southern soldier from capture when he returned home to see his loved ones.

No soldier in Loudoun or Fauquier Counties ever feared that his or his neighbour's servants would betray him to the enemy. The negro always said, in speaking of the Southern soldiers, "our soldiers," although he well knew that the success of the North meant his freedom, while the success of the South meant the continuation of slavery.

Another remarkable thing. No one ever heard of a negro slave, or, so far as I know, a free negro of the South, offering an insult or an indignity to a white woman. They were frequently commissioned to escort the daughters of the family to church or to school, or on any expedition taking them from home. Sometimes the distance was long and across fields and through lonely woods, but the kinky-headed, pigeon-heeled coloured man always delivered his charge safely, and would have died in his footsteps to do it if the occasion required. Freedom, education, or both, or something else, has developed in the negro a trait that no one ever dreamed he possessed until after the close of the Civil War. Hence, I have a great respect for the race. Not, however, on account of this lately-developed trait, but for those other traits that were so much in evidence during the time that tried men's souls.

The following is the name of the several divisions of the army in which I served, and the names of the chief of each division from the captain of my company to the commander-in-chief of the army:

Company.—I was in Company A, first commanded by Col. Richard H. Dulaney, who served a few months and was promoted. He was succeeded by Bruce Gibson of Fauquier County, Virginia, who served during the entire war, and was once knocked from his horse by the concussion of a shell, but sustained no other injuries. Was a prisoner from June, 1864, to the end of the war.

Regiment.—Sixth Virginia Cavalry, commanded first by ex-Governor Flournoy, who served one year, retired on account of age, was succeeded by his son, who was killed at Cold Harbor in June, 1864, and was succeeded by Richards from Clark County, Virginia. The regiment was composed of ten companies, and came from the following counties: Loudoun, Fauquier, Clark and Prince William.

Brigade.—First; Robinson, and then Gen. Wm. E. Jones, who was killed; then Gen. Lomax, who, I believe, is still living near Warrenton, Fauquier County, Virginia.

Division.—Gen. Fitzhugh Lee, nephew of Gen. Robert E. Lee. He survived the war, and died a few months ago.

Corps.—Commanded by Gen. J.E.B. Stuart, who was killed at Yellow Tavern in 1864. He was succeeded by Gen. Wade Hampton of South Carolina, who survived the war and died a few years ago.

Army.—Northern Virginia; commanded first by Gen. P.G.T. Beauregard[2], who was succeeded by Joseph E. Johnston, who was succeeded by Gen. Robert E. Lee, who held the position until the close of the war. Lee was also made commander-in-chief of all the Confederate armies.

---

2. *The Art of War* containing two accounts by Sun Tzu and Pierre G. T. Beauregard, also published by Leonaur.

CHAPTER 11

An After-Thought

The Horses.
Here lies the steed with his nostril all wide,
But through it there rolls not the breath of his pride.
The foam of his gasping lies white on the turf,
And as cold as the spray of the rock-beaten surf.

I do not mean to intimate by the headline of this chapter that I forgot the horses of Lee's army. They were on my mind all through the story, but it was not until the manuscript was in the hands of the printer that the thought came to me that they should have a chapter in this book. Ah! the horses—the blacks and bays, the roans and grays, the sorrels and chestnuts that pulled Lee's army from the Rappahannock to Gettysburg and back, and all the other horses that pulled and tugged at the wagons, at the batteries of artillery; the horses that carried the men, the unstabled horses and the half-fed horses. Let my right hand forget its cunning if I forget to pay proper tribute to those noble animals that suffered so much for their masters.

How often my mind goes back to that horse that I saw coming across the field from the front at Bull Run with his sides all dripping with blood. He was a hero, for he had been out "where the fields were shot, sown and bladed thick with steel," and was coming back to die. Nearly all the bodies of the men were buried, and some horses, for sanitary purposes, were covered with earth, and a few may now be lying in comfortable graves, marked by marble shafts. Lee's gray horse, "Traveller," and Jackson's little

BISHOP ALPHEUS W. WILSON,
Who trained Rover.

sorrel, though dead, may yet be seen, not unlike they were when they bore their riders along the battle front. But the bones of all the other horses that perished whitened for a while the hills and valleys and the roadsides that stretched from Gettysburg to Appomattox, and then when the war was over, men gathered them up and ground them into merchandise to enrich their coffers. The horses that were alive at the close of the war were, for the most part, tenderly cared for, and have long ago joined their comrades on the other side. I hope they are all grazing together on red-headed clover in the green fields of Eden.

How many horses were in Lee's army from beginning to end and how many perished has never been told. Some idea can be formed from the following statement:

Such an army as Lee's, of 100,000 men, required 15,000 draft horses, 10,000 for cavalry, and perhaps 1500 to 2000 for the officers, their staffs and couriers, making a total of 27,000 horses. Perhaps a fair estimate of the number of horses employed in the army of Northern Virginia, commanded by Gen. Lee in person, from 1861 to 1865, would be 75,000. Of these, 30,000 may have survived the war, the remaining 45,000 perished. Add to these, say, 120,000 for the Union army, and we have the sum total of 195,000 horses that took part in that great drama, where the soil of Virginia was the stage.

My first horse was named Rover. She and I were colts together on the farm, I nine years her senior. I loved her, but there are doubts about her love for me. When young, she could run faster, jump higher and cut more "monkey shines" than any colt in the neighbourhood. More than once she landed me on my back in the middle of the road. This was before she entered the military service of the Confederacy.

Once my father was on her back crossing a stream. He loosened the rein to let her drink. A leaf came floating down the stream as peacefully as a summer zephyr. This gave Rover an opportunity for playing one of her pet tricks. When the leaf came in view she pretended to be terribly frightened, made a leap forward, and landed my father on his back in the middle of the stream. The water furnished so soft a bed that he was unhurt. There was a carriage just behind in which Bishop Alpheus W. Wilson of the M.E. Church South, now living in Baltimore, was riding. I heard him tell the story a short time ago, and from the pleasure with which he related it, I am satisfied that he greatly enjoyed the episode at the time, and the remembrance still affords him amusement. The good bishop was then a circuit rider on Loudoun Circuit, and Rover carried him on her back around the circuit. He tried hard to make her a good saddle-horse, and succeeded. He also tried to improve her manners, and while she may have behaved herself when under his eye, it is doubtful whether she ever experienced a change of heart.

I was always suspicious of her, and I had a right to be. Sometimes I thought she was opposed to secession and worked in the interest of the Union. Once she delivered me into the hands of the Yankees, and tried to do it again and again. She seemed to have an affinity for United States horses, and always wanted to carry me directly in among them. It has already been stated that she had a jaw that no bit could hold. If she had been a woman we might have thought that it was the result of talking too much. My, what a weapon of destruction Samson could have made of her jawbone! I don't know when and where she joined the great majority, for we parted company in the spring of 1863 on the banks of the Shenandoah River. I deserted her to avoid capture. We never met again, unless it was on the opposite sides of the battle line, and if so, she took very good care to keep on her own side; at least on the side that was opposed to my side. It grieved me very much to part with her, for, with all her faults, I loved her still.

The cavalryman and his horse got very close to each other, not only physically, but heart to heart. They ate together, slept together, marched, fought and often died together. Frequently a wounded horse would be seen bearing his wounded rider back from the front. During Lee's march to Gettysburg and back the cavalryman was in touch with his horse 18 hours out of 24, and the other six hours he was usually close enough to mount at a moment's warning. Much of the time, while in Pennsylvania, the men slept with their horses tied to the wrist. While the rider slept, the horse cropped the grass around him as far out as his tether would allow him, and as close up to his rider's body as he could get. Sometimes he would push the man's head aside with his nose to get the grass beneath it. I have seen men by the thousands lying in this manner in the fields with their horses grazing about them, yet I never knew a horse to tread on one, or in any way injure him.

On one occasion, near Chambersburg, Pa., the men were sleeping with their horses grazing about them, when the bugle called us to mount. Sometime after forming in line I missed one of my messmates, and called the captain's attention to it. He sent me out over the fields in search of him. I found him just over the crest of a little hill fast asleep, with his horse tied to his wrist. He was lying at full length on his back. His horse had closely cropped the grass all around him, and as far out as he could reach, and so completely had he taken every spear of grass about the soldier that when he got up he left a perfect outline of his body on the field.

On another occasion, when *en route* for Gettysburg, we had halted for a rest at Delaplane, Va. Having no food for our horses we were ordered to turn them loose in the fields to graze. It was 10 o'clock at night. We unbridled and unsaddled our steeds and let them go free. This was in June, and the clover was fine. The hungry animals went briskly to work satisfying their hunger. The grinding of their many jaws sounded like the muffled roar of a distant cataract, and this was the music that lulled the weary men to sleep as they lay scattered over the fields, without any fear of being hurt or trodden upon.

But suppose Kilpatrick had suddenly appeared upon the scene and had thrown a few shells into those fields? What would have been the result? You can trust a horse so far and no farther. A field full of unbridled and frightened horses might have brought death and destruction, and swept Stuart's cavalrymen from the face of the earth. But no such fatality occurred. About

2 o'clock in the morning the bugle sounded "saddle up," and although it was quite dark, in an incredibly short time every man was mounted on his own horse and on the march.

There were times when the cavalry would march all night. The men soon learned to sleep on horseback, or you might call it nodding, but some went sound asleep sitting upright on their horses. Occasionally, when a soldier was caught fast asleep, his comrade would slip the rein out of his hand and lead his horse to a fence corner and hitch it. The sudden stopping would awaken him, for he would at once begin to fall. Catching himself, he would look around in amazement, and if the night were dark, he had no little difficulty finding his place in the ranks.

Little episodes similar to this would help to while away the weary hours of the night. Then there was always some wit or wag, who, at intervals of an hour or so, would arouse the whole line with some ridiculous outburst. A dark and stormy night always called for something extraordinary in this line in order to keep the men in good cheer. After, say an hour of silence, during which time not a sound could be heard save the clatter of the horses' feet, the rattle of the soldiers' armour and the splatter of the rain, when suddenly someone with the voice of a foghorn would rouse up and yell out, "I want to go h-o-m-e, and I am sick, that's what I want."

Then some other fellow far up or down the line would answer back, "I want to see my m-o-t-h-e-r, and I am hungry, too, that's what I want." This was said in a sobbing tone, as if the speaker were about to burst into tears. It would set the whole column off, and for half an hour or so there would be a lively time.

If we were passing a residence, either humble or stately, someone would halt in front of it and "Hello" until he saw a window-sash go up and a head poked out, with the usual question "What is it you want?"

The reply would be, "Say, Mister, you had better take your chimney in, it's going to rain." Then before the angry countryman could get his gun the fun-maker would gallop off to his place in the ranks. And thus the night was passed.

No amount of hardship or deprivation seemed to dampen the ardour of the cavalier. He always had resources, and when in need, they were drawn upon; but the horse, like Felix, cared for none of these things. They seemed to say, "Have all the fun you want, boys, it doesn't disturb us, but don't forget that when we have crossed the river there will be something more serious for you to do; we are following the feather of Stuart tonight." And thus they would trudge on; it mattered not whether storm or calm, they moved in silence, each horse following the one in front of him, or yielding to the gentle pressure of the rein if the rider had occasion to leave the ranks.

Of course, this condition applied only when they were not in proximity to the enemy. When the bluecoats were about things were different. Every man had his horse well in hand; the spur and the rein told the horse where he must go; the men were silent; only the officers spoke.

The horses were fairly well supplied with food until after Gettysburg. Then when winter came and there was no grass and no growing grain, food for Lee's 27,000 horses became a serious problem. I have pulled dried grass in December for my horse until my fingers bled. At other times, when food was more plentiful, the horse was required to share his food with his master, particularly in roasting-ear time. Then our rations were often the same. We cooked ours, while the horse took his green. But during the winter months, when we needed some kind of beverage to wash down our hardtack, the only thing we could get was horse feed, which was roasted and boiled. We called it coffee. It was very good then. We had to rob our horses for this, and we all felt mean when we did it. A table-spoonful, however, was all that each man had to take from his horse for a cup of coffee. The following winter food got scarcer and scarcer for both man and beast, and the horses became thinner and thinner.

I do not know how others felt about the bodies of the dead horses that lay scattered over the battlefields, but this sight distressed me almost as much as did the bodies of the soldiers. They were so faithful and unfaltering. When the bugle sounded, any hour of the night, or any hour of the day, regardless of how short a time they had rested or how many miles they had marched, they were always ready to respond. They knew all the bugle calls. If it were saddle up, or the feed or the water call, he was as ready to answer one as the other. And he was so noble and so brave in battle. He seemed to love the sound of the guns. The cavalryman might lie low on the neck of his horse for shelter as the missiles of death hissed about him, but the horse never flinched, except when struck.

The cavalryman often used his horse for a breastwork while he fired over his back, but the horse stood like a Casabianca on the burning deck of his father's ship. Did you ever read *Black Beauty?* If you have not, read it. Lee had 75,000 "Black Beauties" in his army, every one of which, or nearly every one, is worthy of a monument. We build monuments for our dead soldiers, for those we know and for the unknown dead. What would you think of a monument some day, somewhere in Virginia, in honour of Lee's noble horses?

I hardly know which branch of the service ought to receive the highest honour, the wagon horses, the artillery horses or the cavalry horses. I was very close to the latter, and knew them better, but the wagon and artillery horses had a warm place in my heart. To see the wagon horses hitched to heavy, loaded wagons, with shells falling around them, with no way of escape, was pathetic. To see the artillery horses torn to pieces by shells that were not intended for them touched a tender cord, and if I should be asked to write their names on the roll of fame, perhaps it would be in the order in which I have named them.

The cavalry horse, however, was my pet, and I should not want to see them any less honoured than the former, but they all had their places. Farragut, in the rigging of his flagship giving orders, was all right, but a wooden Indian would have done about as well if the coal-shoveller below had failed to do his duty. What could Gen. Lee have done had all his horses balked in unison? Nothing. Then all honour to Lee's horses, who pulled and hauled and fought and died that this might be a very great nation.

No more appropriate lines could be had for the ending of this story than the following touching little poem by Francis Alexander Durivage:

There hangs a sabre, and there a rein,
With a rusty buckle and green curb chain;
A pair of spurs on the old gray wall,
And a mouldy saddle—well, that is all.

Come out to the stable—it is not far;
The moss-grown door is hanging ajar.
Look within! There's an empty stall,
Where once stood a charger, and that is all.

The good black horse came riderless home,
Flecked with blood drops as well as foam;
See yonder hillock where dead leaves fall;
The good black horse dropped dead—that is all.

All? O, God! it is all I can speak.
Question me not, I am old and weak;
His sabre and his saddle hang on the wall,
And his horse is dead—I have told you all.

NOTE.—I said in the beginning that I had not consulted any of the Civil War histories for material for this book. After the manuscript was in type, I read for the first time James Longstreet's book on the Civil War; also Henderson's *Life of Jackson*, and I am indebted to these two authors for some facts in regard to the losses in battle and the number engaged. To the latter I am indebted for the tragic account of the wounding and death of Stonewall Jackson. These additions are mostly to be found in foot notes throughout the book.